From Frazzled To Focused

OrangeBooks Publication

1st Floor, Rajhans Arcade, Mall Road, Kohka, Bhilai, Chhattisgarh 490020

Website: **www.orangebooks.in**

© Copyright, 2024, Author

All rights reserved. No part of this book may be reproduced, stored in a retrieval system, or transmitted, in any form by any means, electronic, mechanical, magnetic, optical, chemical, manual, photocopying, recording or otherwise, without the prior written consent of its writer.

First Edition, 2024

ISBN: 978-93-6554-161-8

FROM FRAZZLED TO FOCUSED

PREETI JOSHI

OrangeBooks Publication
www.orangebooks.in

*Dedicating this book to my PARENTS
will always be grateful to you
and in gratitude*

Acknowledgement

Writing "Frazzled to Focused" has been a journey of exploration and growth. It wouldn't have been possible without the support and inspiration of many incredible people.

First and foremost, my heartfelt gratitude goes to:

- **My Parents & Husband:** Their unwavering belief in me and my work, fuelled my motivation throughout this process. Thank you for always being there for me, helping and blessing me

- **My Clients:** Sharing your experiences and struggles with me provided invaluable insights that shaped the content of this book.

Special thanks to:

- Orange Publications who have helped me in publishing my book and have helped in giving insightful suggestions, and constant support helped refine my ideas and make this book a reality.

Finally, a word of gratitude to all the readers: Thank you for picking up this book. I hope that "Frazzled to Focused" empowers you to navigate the challenges of work life with increased focus, inner peace, and a renewed sense of purpose.

With sincere appreciation,

Preeti Joshi

Endorsements

Lokesh Saxena (Managing Director)

The topic of transformation itself draws my attention as I believe, each and every person struggle to implement transformation in true sense in their own lives.

The issues like "procrastination", "building our own brand" and "it starts from self" are captured well in this book. These issues require immense determination and guidance to practise.

This book provides a systematic approach to move into this direction through ways of meditation, brand building, use of Chakras etc.

The author making a connection of "healthy mind and healthy body" to the transformation process is the highlight of this book.

The book captures in true sense the reality of the corporate individuals. The author, being a corporate navigator herself, has captured the reality well including the struggle to deal with the transformation process. The author has used her own story well to depict some real-life situations as well.

I believe that this book will serve as a guide and would encourage the readers to practice the recommendations and enjoy the benefits over a period.

Neeta Thakkur - Banking professional, Poet, Writer, Artist and Cancer Thriver

In her insightful book "From Frazzled to Focused", Preeti Joshi provides a practical and inspiring guide to help readers reclaim their focus and productivity in today's fast-paced world.

She draws from her own life experiences, her deep knowledge of a multitude of sciences, mindfulness and her personal development coaching experience to offer a holistic approach to tackling overwhelming, complex issues and emotional baggage.

One of the strengths of the book is Preeti's simplified explanations emphasizing varied mindfulness techniques and mindset shifts to improve mental clarity and emotional well-being.

She introduces simple yet powerful strategies that readers can implement in their daily lives to manage stress and achieve a greater sense of productivity and balance.

Preeti's writing is engaging and relatable, making it easy for readers to connect with her message and apply the concepts discussed in the book. The anecdotes and life examples peppered throughout the chapters serve to illustrate the effectiveness of her recommended strategies and solutions.

Overall, "From Frazzled to Focused" is a well-rounded guide that offers actionable advice for those seeking to declutter their minds and lead a more purposeful life. Preeti Joshi's wisdom and insights make this book a valuable addition to any personal development library.

Dr. Aparna Joshi

The author, Preeti Joshi has very deftly intertwined subtle components of the human existence and experience and managed to portray it in its entirety and complexity.

The unseen factors which hold together the human psyche and substance, their interconnections and their cumulative impressions on the individual and on the cosmos is fascinating matter for study and contemplation and the author has demonstrated a seamless, systematic symphony to produce divine music together! I suggest this book to everyone interested in understanding the finer nuances of existence and evolution and of being a better version of oneself by implementing the various practical techniques enumerated in the book!

A very HAPPY JOURNEY to all of you!

Ritu Dhiman – HR Head

"Frazzled to Focused" presents in a simple relatable way how to rearrange some necessary aspects of your life. Aptly covered with personal stories and anecdotes this a must read for everyone looking to have some control and focus back in their life

As Preeti puts it," All changes within, will create changes in my outer world ". Use the tools provided in book to bring these changes.

Rekha Kamble Officer in LIC

The title itself is so appropriate that right there, it makes the reader think differently. From Frazzled to Focused

Frazzled – broken, completely shattered, fragmented... Focused – brought together and concentrated. From my perspective, I would say that someone whose life is completely devastated, after reading this book, would regain their original personality, becoming fully integrated inside and out. The book offers such a detailed analysis of human existence and every aspect of it, that the purpose of the book and how it can benefit the reader is felt from the first page to the last.

Every person, at every moment, is under some kind of mental stress, and surely, each of them needs this book. It teaches how to manage your mind, create effective strategic plans, and how to reduce your anxiety and stress. The solutions and treatments provided are especially important in order to achieve a productive state.

According to the author, prioritizing your mental and emotional health can positively impact all other areas of your life. It can help balance your professional and family life. Reading this book and practicing what it teaches can lead to your overall development.

The author has presented these experienced, profound psychological insights with great research. When we approach things with the right perspective – making small changes and learning to question our responses – we can gain a broader vision of life.

In short, the book explains, in an encouraging way, how we can work on the small things that rob us of our mental health, that make us frazzled, and how we can become focused to stop these things from affecting us, regaining control over our lives."

Prashant Shotry - The book is an excellent guide to mental, spiritual, physical wellbeing. Here the author is just not listing the problem, issues faced by an individual but gives practical solutions. The quantum number healing technique, salt uses, switch words just the examples which we normally don't come across in such similar books. The reader of this book if practices techniques elaborated in this book will experience a complete turn in his personality. I congratulate the author for giving such a useful tool for mental, physical wellbeing of people.

Disclaimer

This book is designed for those ready to elevate their energy and unlock the science behind emotions—a courageous leap towards TRANSFORMATION.

Our goal is to reshape your perspective on emotions, energy, and thoughts. By engaging with this book, you'll cultivate a positive mindset and lay a strong foundation rooted in empowering thoughts.

Take your time, absorb the techniques, and watch yourself transform into a highly productive individual.

Embrace the journey—Be the Change.

Index

Introduction The Productivity Paradox 1

From Engineering Dreams to Healing Realities: My Story 4

You Are The Universe 9

Your Mind 19

Power Words for Daily Transformation 91

The Productivity Boost in Every Drop 124

Help Others 128

Connect With The Author 133

Testimonies 134

Introduction
The Productivity Paradox

Welcome, busy professional! Are you constantly juggling deadlines, feeling overwhelmed by your workload, and struggling to maintain focus? If so, you're not alone. In today's fast-paced work environment, the pressure to be productive can often hinder our ability to achieve it. This pressure, coupled with the demands of managing both home and office, can take a serious toll on your emotional, mental, and physical health.

This book introduces a powerful approach to breaking free from this cycle. By addressing the emotional factors that contribute to stress and anxiety, you can unlock new levels of focus, clarity, and productivity. The journey of "From Frazzled to Focused" is about developing emotional healing alongside practical tools to empower you to thrive in your career.

The Importance of Mindset

As an astrologer and astro-numerologist, I've studied how mindset influences our lives. Astrology and numerology reveal the qualities you are born with and can develop, and how to work on traits that hinder your progress, such as indecisiveness, poor communication skills, or negative thinking.

Many people seek quick fixes, hoping for magic solutions. However, real change comes from within. Success is 80% mindset and 20% skill set. Understanding and working on your limiting beliefs is crucial, as the universe operates on simple principles: "As you sow, so shall you reap."

Understanding Brain States and Healing

Your current mental state greatly affects your productivity. Let's explore four types of brain waves:

1. Beta State: An overactive mind filled with self-talk and noise, leading to missed opportunities, poor decisions, and increased stress.

2. Alpha State: A relaxed mind, ideal for creativity and attracting opportunities. This state can be achieved through mindfulness and meditation.

3. Theta State: A deeper meditative state where profound healing occurs. This state can help overcome emotional and physical challenges.

4. Delta State: The deepest meditative state, conducive to complete rest and profound healing.

The Power of Water Memory

Dr. Masaru Emoto, a Japanese scientist, demonstrated that water has memory. Positive thoughts can create beautiful, healthy patterns in water, while negative thoughts can create harmful patterns. Since our bodies are mostly water, our thoughts significantly impact our health. Healing major health challenges requires faith and time.

Your Journey Begins Here

This book is not just another self-help guide; it's a roadmap for transforming from a frazzled professional to a focused and thriving individual. By prioritizing your well-being and implementing the strategies in this book, you can achieve calm control, unlock your potential, and experience the joy of focused productivity.

Remember, success is not the key to happiness. Happiness is the key to success. Embrace the practices that work for you, seek additional support if needed, and enjoy your transformation journey.

From Engineering Dreams to Healing Realities: My Story

In 1975, my father relocated our family to the vibrant city of Davangere, Karnataka. Everything was new—the places, the people, the language. As a fearless and confident child, I thrived on making new friends and exploring the world beyond the confines of books, much to my parents' chagrin. My mischievous antics often led to complaints from school and neighbours, and my father, concerned about my future, nicknamed me "DON'T CARE MASTER."

A turning point came when my elder sister graduated as an Electronics Engineer. Her success and the pride she exuded inspired me to take my studies seriously. Despite my father's scepticism, I surprised everyone, including myself, by securing commendable marks in the 10th grade. In 1985, driven by a newfound sense of purpose, I announced my desire to become a Chef—a passion that filled me with joy. My father, however, dismissed my dream, insisting I pursue a Diploma in Computer Science, believing it to be the best path to success.

Reluctantly, I embarked on this journey, completing my Diploma with first-class honour's in 1989. Determined to build a stable career, I chose to pursue engineering and secured a seat at Bapuji Institute of Engineering in

Davangere. That same year, my father moved to Mumbai for work, leaving me to navigate the challenges of hostel life and subpar food, which often made me ill.

In 1992, an accident during my 5th-semester exams resulted in a fractured leg, forcing me to take a year off. Despite this setback, I completed my Engineering degree in 1994 and moved to Mumbai to join my family. Adjusting to life in a bustling metropolis was daunting, especially navigating the crowded local trains. Mumbai, with its endless opportunities and fierce competition, demanded resilience and adaptability.

With unwavering confidence, I printed my resume and began promoting myself, going door-to-door in an industrial estate in search of a job. In September 1994, I landed my first position at a programming company, earning a modest salary of Rs 1000. My father's mantra, "Time and tide wait for none," was deeply ingrained in my mind, driving me to believe that perseverance and hard work would lead to success. However, my interest in programming was fleeting, and I soon found myself drawn to the dynamic field of supply chain management.

In 1999, I joined a Swiss organization as an Assistant Manager, overseeing order management. My focus, confidence, and leadership skills propelled me forward, yet it took time to master the nuances of corporate life and the importance of emotional resilience. Throughout my career, I discovered several KEY LESSONS ESSENTIAL FOR PROFESSIONAL GROWTH:

- Self-Change: True influence begins within; we can only change ourselves.

- Emotional Mastery: Emotions are the greatest adversary in the professional world; healing them is crucial for success.
- Positive Mindset: A positive outlook is vital for achieving goals.
- Personal Goals: Defining personal goals helps identify necessary changes and knowledge for success.
- Relationship Management: Workplace relationships must be navigated wisely.
- No Complaints: Never complain.
- Observation Over Reaction: Be an observer; avoid reacting or retaliating.
- Communication: Effective communication is key to success.
- Work Focus: Everyone is at work to work, not to make friends.
- Emotional Control: Don't dwell on emotions; they can be used against you.

Applying these principles helped me thrive in various roles over 18 years. After successfully leading **All-India customer service, I decided in 2016** to pursue my passion. When I informed my parents of my decision to leave my corporate career for metaphysics, they were concerned but ultimately supportive, giving me their blessings.

Teaching and coaching became my new focus. I immersed myself in various healing and predictive sciences like numerology, astrology, Reiki, Akashic reading, auto-writing, and graphology. These fields captivated me, and I approached them scientifically. As a Reiki Grandmaster and Akashic Reader, I gained profound insights into healing, understanding the root causes of illnesses, and how emotions create challenges that can be healed.

In March 2016, I was diagnosed with a cataract in my right eye. The doctor scheduled surgery for November, but I chose to heal myself through daily meditation and Reiki. Remarkably, after three months, my cataract began to dissolve, and within six months, it was 99% gone. My doctor was astonished, acknowledging the power of healing. I similarly healed my frozen shoulder and spondylitis within just 45 days.

Throughout my 21 years in the corporate world, I never sought the guidance of astrologers or occult practitioners. My interest in these subjects was rooted in understanding their scientific basis and guiding people accordingly. With the help of great teachers, I realized that predictive sciences serve as guiding lights, helping us comprehend our capabilities, challenges, and areas for improvement.

Consistent self-work is essential for evolution. I believe that true change comes not from wearing rings or jewellery but from hard work and mental and emotional growth. With over nine years of my coaching and consulting experience, I have coached more than 350 working professionals and mentored over 1,500 individuals. My journey continues with passion, emphasizing the importance of finding and channelling one's inner passion to help others.

You Are The Universe

Did you know that you are part of a universal plan and that the universe reflects your thoughts? Your life is a road map designed by your higher self, and your key challenges are areas where you need to improve.

We Are the Spark: Embracing Shortcomings on the Path to Transformation

Imagine the universe as a vast tapestry, woven with threads of experience, both light and dark. Each thread, every challenge, and every triumph contribute to the intricate design. You, as an individual, are a single strand in this tapestry, your life journey a unique colour woven into the grand scheme.

But what if this isn't just a beautiful metaphor? What if we are all, in essence, part of a universal plan, actively contributing to the evolution of the cosmos? This perspective shifts our understanding of our shortcomings and reframes them as opportunities for growth.

The Imperfect Masterpiece

We are born with a unique set of strengths and weaknesses. These "shortcomings" aren't mistakes but variations in the tapestry. A world woven with only vibrant reds and oranges would lack the depth and complexity of one that incorporates blues, greens, and even the occasional thread of grey.

Our imperfections, our struggles with fear, anxiety, or self-doubt, offer valuable lessons. They push us to develop resilience, empathy, and a deeper understanding of the human experience. Overcoming these challenges strengthens the threads in our tapestry, making them more vibrant and resilient.

The Journey of Transformation

The universal plan doesn't demand perfection; it yearns for our constant evolution. Every experience, positive or negative, shapes our perspective and expands our capacity for love, compassion, and understanding. We are not static beings but ever-evolving souls on a journey towards a more positive, amplified version of ourselves.

This transformation isn't linear. There will be setbacks, moments when the dark threads seem dominant. But that's part of the process. Just as a storm reveals the strength of a mighty oak, challenging experiences reveal the depths of our resilience. The key is to embrace the journey, with its twists and turns, and learn from each step.

Harnessing the Power of Positivity

While acknowledging our shortcomings, we must also cultivate an unwavering sense of optimism. Positivity isn't about ignoring challenges; it's about approaching them with a belief in our ability to overcome them. This positive energy acts like a bright thread woven into the tapestry, illuminating the path towards transformation.

Positivity doesn't mean blind optimism. It's about acknowledging the darkness while focusing on the light within ourselves and the world. It's about finding beauty even in the cracks, nurturing hope even in the face of adversity. By amplifying this positive energy, we contribute to the collective good and empower others to do the same.

Weaving the Tapestry Together

We are not isolated strands in the tapestry; we are interconnected. Our actions, choices, and transformations impact the lives of others. By embracing our shortcomings and striving to be positive, amplified versions of ourselves, we create a ripple effect of positive change. We inspire others to confront their own challenges and weave their unique threads into the grand tapestry with greater strength and purpose.

The Part We Play

So, the next time you feel discouraged by your shortcomings, remember this: you are an essential part of a universal plan. Embrace your flaws, learn from your experiences, and cultivate a sense of unwavering optimism. By doing so, you are not just transforming yourself; you are contributing to the beauty and complexity of the grand cosmic tapestry, thread by precious thread.

Your repeated challenges in life indicate that you are ignoring certain important lessons. By learning these lessons, you can create shifts in your life. For example, if a person wants to sell an item or equipment, they need to know the entire selling strategy and have strong communication skills. Without these, they might fall into a loop of failures and feel dejected.

The Power to Change Realities

Have you ever introspected on how you can change your realities? Have you heard of people who were born very poor but later excelled in life and helped their families out of poverty? Understand that you are the God or Divine of your universe, capable of shaping your own reality. It's crucial to observe yourself and your thoughts. If you tend to be emotionally hurt and withdrawn and always think others need to change, you need to shift your perspective, as we can only change ourselves.

I always say, "ALL CHANGES WITHIN, WILL CREATE CHANGES IN MY OUTER WORLD"

– *Preeti Joshi.*

It is crucial to understand that you attract everything based on your thoughts and emotions.

The Importance of Inner Work

During my coaching sessions, I encountered individuals who had traumatic childhoods. One client was stuck in a trauma that happened at age 11. Despite being 28, he was still grieving, creating self-judgments, losing opportunities, and living a miserable life. It's crucial to work on our inner emotions, hurt, grief, or trauma to embrace the goodness life or the universe has to offer.

Have you ever had colleagues or friends mention that you ignored them, even though you were just engrossed in your thoughts? This happens because we tend to judge people and create our own interpretations of what others might be thinking.

Judgments and Misinterpretations

In one coaching session, a client mentioned that his colleague thought he was a loser and didn't do his job well. I asked if his colleague had ever expressed this, and he admitted it was just his assumption. This is a common situation where our minds create judgments and misinterpretations.

By confronting these judgments, my client was able to free himself from them and improve his networking and social interactions. The universe is a mirror, reflecting our judgments and actions. Instead of pointing fingers at others, we need to look within and quiet our judgments. This allows for constructive actions rather than destructive ones.

The Power of Our Aura

We all have invisible antennas that transmit and receive feelings and emotions from our aura. The aura, an electromagnetic field surrounding our body, stores energy in terms of emotions, trauma, and grief. It can extend up to 4 to 5 meters from the body and even further for those practicing meditation and spirituality.

It's said that predictions cannot be made for those on a strong spiritual path, as they have mastered the art of living and remain unaffected by challenges. If an astrologer predicts a challenging episode for a spiritual person, they may decline it, stating that everything is happy and joyous because they have learned to stay in a state of zero.

The Impact of Negative Thoughts

If you hold a negative thought about someone, your invisible antennas transmit this information, and the person starts behaving in the way you envisioned. You then think you knew how they would react, not realizing you influenced their behaviour.

It's important to work on your emotions and avoid letting your emotional **self-created castles control you**. By doing so, you can change your reality and improve your interactions with others.

The idea that the universe is a reflection of our thoughts is rooted in various philosophical, spiritual, and metaphysical traditions. This concept suggests that our inner world of thoughts, beliefs, and emotions directly influences and shapes our external reality. Here are several perspectives that explore this intriguing notion:

1. Law of Attraction

Basic Principle: The Law of Attraction posits that like attracts like, meaning that the thoughts and feelings we focus on are reflected back to us in our experiences. Positive thoughts and emotions attract positive outcomes, while negative ones attract negative outcomes.

Manifestation: This principle is often associated with the practice of manifestation, where individuals consciously cultivate positive thoughts and visualize desired outcomes to bring them into reality. Techniques such as affirmations, visualization, and gratitude practices are commonly used.

2. Quantum Physics and Consciousness

Observer Effect: In quantum physics, the observer effect suggests that the act of observing a particle can influence its state. Some interpretations of this phenomenon propose that consciousness itself plays a role in shaping reality.

To better understand the observer effect, let's explore an example: after watching a horror, sad, action, or aggressive movie, you will likely carry that energy with you for some time. This is true unless you watch the movie with a complete sense of detachment, viewing it purely as entertainment. Similarly, if you are surrounded by positive individuals, you will also be influenced by their energy.

Quantum Entanglement

Quantum entanglement describes how particles can become interconnected and instantaneously affect each other, regardless of distance. This phenomenon has led some to speculate the interconnectedness of all things and the potential influence of consciousness on the universe.

For Example, consider a situation where you think of a friend and, just as you're about to call them, they call you. This experience, often referred to as telepathy, highlights a form of seemingly synchronous connection that mirrors the ideas of quantum entanglement, suggesting a deeper interconnectedness that might influence our interactions.

3. Psychology and Perception

Cognitive Psychology: Cognitive psychology examines how our thoughts and beliefs influence our perceptions and behaviour's. Cognitive-behavioural therapy (CBT) focuses on identifying and changing negative thought patterns to alter emotional responses and behaviours.

For Example, if a person is involved in too much of negative self-talk he would be creating a shield which will not permit him to look for opportunities and also seek help. The CBT system will provide the individual techniques to come of this loop and empower Self to become more focused on positive aspects of life.

4. Self-Fulfilling Prophecies

A self-fulfilling prophecy occurs when a person's expectations about a situation or outcome influence their behaviour in a way that causes those expectations to come true. This highlights the power of belief in shaping reality.

Many visionaries use this technique to create an empire, It is very essential to create your brand in your professional & personal life. You need to set personal targets in order to achieve your personal goals. Only if you strive for this you will see accomplishing your goals and shaping your reality.

5. Spiritual and Mystical Perspectives

Mystical traditions across cultures often describe experiences of unity with the cosmos, where the boundaries between self and the universe dissolve.

Mystics report that their inner states and realizations are reflected in their perception of the external world.

It is very crucial to ensure that you be in Alpha state than being in Beta state, if you seek changes in your personal reality you need to ensure your inner talk is positive.

New Thought Movement

- The New Thought movement, which emerged in the 19th century, emphasizes the power of the mind to influence physical reality. It teaches that thoughts are a form of energy that can manifest as physical experiences.

6. Practical Implications

Personal Growth

- Believing that the universe reflects our thoughts can encourage individuals to take responsibility for their inner states and cultivate positive, empowering beliefs. This perspective can be a catalyst for personal growth and transformation.

Mindfulness and Intentionality

- Practices such as mindfulness, meditation, and positive affirmations help individuals become more aware of their thoughts and direct them in ways that align with their desired outcomes.

Interconnectedness

- Recognizing the potential interconnectedness between our inner and outer worlds fosters a sense of unity and empathy. It encourages individuals to cultivate compassion and positive intentions, contributing to a more harmonious collective reality.

Your Mind

The Unseen Powerhouse: Mastering Your Mind for Positivity and Amplification

Imagine yourself standing before a vast, intricate control panel. Countless dials, switches, and levers represent the workings of a magnificent machine: your mind. This unseen powerhouse governs your thoughts, emotions, and actions, shaping your reality and influencing everything you do. Understanding how your mind works is the key to unlocking its immense potential for positivity and amplification.

The Symphony of Thoughts:

Our minds function through a constant flow of neural activity. Sensory information bombards us incessantly, triggering the firing of neurons and the creation of thought patterns. These patterns, both positive and negative, can become ingrained over time, solidifying into neural pathways that dictate our behaviour and decision-making.

The Duality of Perception:

It's important to understand that our perception of reality isn't a simple reflection of the world around us. It's a nuanced blend of external stimuli filtered through our internal lenses of beliefs, experiences, and emotions. For example, someone with a history of negativity might interpret a neutral event as a personal attack, while someone with a positive outlook might see the same situation as an opportunity.

The Impact of Point of View on an Individual

Our point of view, or the way we perceive and interpret the world around us, plays a crucial role in shaping our thoughts, behaviour's, and overall life experiences. This perspective, influenced by our upbringing, culture, personal experiences, and even biological factors, can profoundly affect various aspects of our lives, from our mental health to our relationships and professional success. Here, we delve into how point of view impacts an individual and why it's important to cultivate a positive and open-minded perspective.

Our point of view shapes our reality. It influences how we interpret our experiences, interact with others, approach challenges, and perceive our own abilities. By cultivating a positive, open-minded perspective, we can enhance our mental and emotional well-being, build stronger relationships, achieve professional success, and navigate life's challenges more effectively. It's important to be mindful of our point of view and to actively work on reshaping it, if necessary, through practices such as mindfulness, cognitive-behavioural techniques, and seeking diverse perspectives. In doing so, we can transform our lives and unlock our full potential.

Shaping Your Reality: Rejecting Scarcity Mindset

Have you ever encountered a colleague who approaches you with a specific, often negative point of view? For example, in many work environments, someone might say, "The market is slow, and there are no jobs out there." This is their point of view, and by expressing it, they are creating a reality based on this belief.

The Power of Belief

If you agree with them and internalize this perspective, you become part of their reality. The universe will start manifesting this scarcity situation in your life as well. Instead of agreeing, it's essential to remind yourself to shut down these negative thoughts. Avoid engaging in such conversations and move away from these situations.

Abundance Mindset

Scarcity is created in people's minds. The universe is infinite and abundant; there is no inherent lack. The perceived lack is in our thoughts, and we must consciously avoid discussions that reinforce this mindset. By abandoning thoughts of scarcity and embracing an abundance mindset, you align yourself with the infinite possibilities the universe offers.

Shifting Perspectives

The next time someone expresses a limiting belief, remember that it is just their perspective. You have the power to choose your reality. Focus on abundance, reject scarcity, and watch as the universe manifests prosperity and opportunities in your life.

The Habit Machine:

Our brains, in their quest for efficiency, favour established neural pathways. This is why positive or negative thought patterns can become habitual. If you constantly dwell on negativity, these pathways become stronger, making it more challenging to cultivate a positive mindset.

Examples in Action:

Let's delve into a few practical examples to illustrate these concepts:

- **The Self-Fulfilling Prophecy:** Consider someone who constantly worries about failing at work. This anxiety manifests as a lack of confidence, leading to actual performance issues. These issues then reinforce the initial negative thought pattern, creating a self-fulfilling prophecy.

- **The Power of Gratitude:** Practicing gratitude by focusing on the good things in life strengthens positive neural pathways. When you appreciate what you have, the brain starts searching for more positive experiences, creating a virtuous cycle.

- **The Reframing Game:** Challenging negative thoughts and reframing them in a more positive light can disrupt negative patterns. A missed promotion might be reframed as an opportunity to learn new skills or explore new career paths. This shift in perspective fosters a sense of empowerment instead of defeat.

- **The Power of Visualization:** Imagine a world-class athlete visualizing success before a competition. This visualization activates similar neural pathways as actually experiencing victory, strengthening belief and motivation. By harnessing this power, we can amplify our potential in any area of life.

Mental Health and Emotional Well-being

The point of view we hold can significantly affect our mental health and emotional well-being. Individuals with a positive outlook on life are more likely to experience higher levels of happiness and lower levels of stress. They tend to focus on the good in situations and people, which fosters resilience and a sense of gratitude. Conversely, a negative point of view can lead to increased anxiety, depression, and a sense of helplessness. For example, someone who views challenges as insurmountable obstacles is more likely to feel overwhelmed and discouraged, while someone who sees them as opportunities for growth is likely to approach them with enthusiasm and confidence.

Relationships

Our point of view also influences our relationships with others. People who see the world through a lens of trust and openness are more likely to form healthy, supportive relationships. They tend to give others the benefit of the doubt, communicate openly, and resolve conflicts constructively. On the other hand, a cynical or distrustful perspective can lead to isolation, misunderstandings, and conflict. If an individual constantly expects others to let them down or hurt them, they may become defensive, overly critical, or withdrawn, which can strain or sever relationships.

Professional Success

In the professional realm, point of view can be a determining factor in success. A proactive and optimistic mindset can drive an individual to set ambitious goals, take initiative, and persevere in the face of setbacks. Such individuals are often seen as leaders and innovators, as they inspire others and are willing to take risks to achieve their objectives. In contrast, a pessimistic or defeatist attitude can hinder career advancement. Employees who view their work environment negatively may lack motivation, resist change, and miss opportunities for growth and improvement.

Problem-Solving and Creativity

An individual's perspective also affects their problem-solving abilities and creativity. Those who adopt a growth mindset, believing that abilities and intelligence can be developed, are more likely to think outside the box and find innovative solutions to problems. They are open to feedback and willing to experiment with new ideas. Conversely, a fixed mindset can stifle creativity and problem-solving. If someone believes that their abilities are static and that failure is a reflection of their limitations, they may avoid challenges and stick to familiar, safe solutions.

Coping with Adversity

How we cope with adversity is greatly influenced by our point of view. Individuals with a resilient mindset see adversity as a temporary setback and a natural part of life. They are more likely to use adaptive coping strategies, such as seeking support, problem-solving, and maintaining a hopeful outlook. This perspective enables them to bounce back from difficulties and continue pursuing their goals. In contrast, a more negative or fatalistic viewpoint can lead to maladaptive coping mechanisms, such as avoidance, denial, or substance abuse, which can exacerbate stress and impede recovery.

Taking Charge of Your Mental Landscape:

The good news is that we are not prisoners to our thoughts. While our minds are powerful, we can actively work to cultivate a more positive and amplified state. Here are some practical steps to take charge of your mental landscape:

- **Mindfulness Practices:** Meditation, deep breathing exercises, and other mindfulness techniques can help you become aware of your thoughts and emotions without judgment. By observing your thoughts, you can choose how you react instead of being controlled by automatic responses.

- **Positive Affirmations:** Repeating positive affirmations about yourself and your capabilities can help rewire your brain for positivity. These affirmations can be simple statements like "I am capable" or "I am worthy of happiness."

- **Gratitude Journaling:** Taking time each day to write down things you're grateful for strengthens positive thought patterns and boosts overall well-being. Studies have shown that gratitude journaling can significantly improve happiness levels.

- **Gratitude Exercises:** Look for opportunities to express gratitude to others, not just for yourself. This fosters positive connections and reinforces a positive outlook, creating a ripple effect of happiness.

- **Limiting Negative Influences:** Identify and minimize negative influences in your life, such as toxic relationships or overly critical news sources. Bombarding your mind with negativity makes it harder to maintain a positive mindset.

- **Surrounding Yourself with Positivity:** Spend time with positive people who uplift and inspire you. Listen to uplifting music, watch funny movies, and engage in activities that bring joy. Creating a positive environment strengthens your positive neural pathways.

Amplifying Your Potential:

By taking charge of your mental landscape and cultivating a positive mindset, you unlock your full potential. You become more resilient, resourceful, and capable of achieving your goals. This amplification extends beyond yourself, as your positive energy inspires and empowers those around you, creating a ripple effect of well-being.

Remember, your mind is an extraordinary tool. By understanding its workings and taking active steps towards positivity, you can transform your reality and amplify your potential to create a happier, more fulfilling life for yourself and those around you. You hold the key to harnessing the unseen powerhouse within, and with dedication and effort, you can unlock its power to create a brighter tomorrow.

The Tripartite Mind: Exploring the Conscious, Subconscious, and Superconscious

Imagine the human mind as a vast iceberg. The tip, visible above the water, represents the conscious mind – the realm of our waking thoughts, perceptions, and decisions. But beneath the surface lies a hidden world, a complex interplay between the subconscious and superconscious minds. Understanding these three layers is key to unlocking our full potential and achieving a state of well-being.

The Conscious Mind: The Stage of Awareness, it is said to be 10% of the entire mind

The conscious mind acts as the director of our waking experience. It processes information from the senses, analyses thoughts and feelings, and guides our actions. It's here that we make decisions, solve problems, and engage in critical thinking.

"The only person you are destined to become is the person you decide to be." - Ralph Waldo Emerson

Exercise: Practice mindfulness meditation. Focus on your breath and observe your thoughts without judgment.

This helps train your conscious mind to be more aware of your inner workings.

The Subconscious Mind: The Powerhouse of Habits, 70% powerful

The subconscious mind is the vast, unseen realm beneath the surface. It houses our memories, beliefs, and learned behaviours. It operates automatically, governing our instincts, habits, and emotional responses. For example, when you ride a bicycle, the conscious mind may have learned how initially, but the subconscious takes over the coordination and movement once mastered.

"The mind is everything. What you think you become." - Buddha

Exercise: Explore journaling. Write down your dreams and recurring thoughts. These can offer valuable insights into your subconscious beliefs and motivations.

The Superconscious Mind: The Realm of Intuition and Creativity, 20%

The superconscious mind, sometimes called the higher self, is the least understood aspect of our tripartite mind. It's associated with intuition, inspiration, and connection to something larger than ourselves. It's the source of creativity, flashes of insight, and feelings of deep connection.

"The intuitive mind is a sacred gift and the rational mind is a faithful servant. We have created a society that honours the servant and has forgotten the gift." - Albert Einstein

Exercise: Practice visualization. Spend time visualizing your goals and aspirations in vivid detail. This can tap into the superconscious mind and empower you to manifest your desires.

The Symphony of the Mind:

These three levels of mind don't operate in isolation; they work together in a beautiful symphony. The conscious mind receives information from the senses and the subconscious, while the superconscious provides inspiration and guidance. Our thoughts, emotions, and actions are all influenced by this dynamic interplay.

Unlocking Your Potential:

By understanding these three levels of mind, we can unlock our full potential. Here are some ways to achieve this:

- **Balancing the Mind:** Integrate practices that address all three levels. Develop your conscious awareness through meditation, nurture your subconscious through affirmations and self-hypnosis, and tap into your superconscious through creative activities and visualization.

- **Reframing Negative Patterns:** The subconscious often holds onto limiting beliefs. Use journaling and therapy to identify negative patterns and reframe them into empowering ones.

- **Harnessing Intuition:** Pay attention to gut feelings and sudden insights. These might be your superconscious mind guiding you in the right direction.

We now have a basic understanding of the mind and its three states. The mind's conscious, subconscious, and subconscious

A few additional thoughts on the subconscious, which is the storehouse of our memories, belief systems, and recurring behaviours.

Because humans are emotional creatures, whenever we revisit a memory or event repeatedly, we are telling our subconscious mind that it is important. The subconscious mind then needs to set alarms whenever it encounters similar circumstances and bring in emotions like fear or anxiety, as well as any limiting beliefs or patterns that we may have developed during the course of the recalled event

I refer to the subconscious mind as a slave because it simply retains information that it is continuously reminded of, recognizes its importance, and stores it in its subconscious reservoir.

It is crucial to remember that as the subconscious mind begins to repeat information, it becomes harder to remove and requires constant mending to restore the memory. Therefore, the next time you experience hurt, emotional trauma, or grief, make sure to begin mending right away to prevent it from being stored in your subconscious mind.

For instance, when someone has endured repeated humiliation at the hands of a management, it can erode their self-esteem and cause them to feel anxious, tense, and afraid. In this instance, if the person retrieves the memory and laments over it for several days, he is generating cloned memory, which will have a profound effect and necessitate enormous effort to heal. Each healing process begins with memory n-1, memory n-2... memory to the power of 1, and ends with the original memory.

As an additional example, have you ever noticed how you react when someone falls on the street? If so, you may panic as though it has happened to you. This communicates to your subconscious mind that you have witnessed this event, find it significant, and want it to happen. You will therefore either trip over or get harmed after a few days or weeks after you have forgotten about this experience, and you won't realize it was this signal you gave your subconscious mind. Think back if you have experienced anything similar.

The question then becomes, "What do we do together when we come across such situations?"

To which I would advise you to respond, **"Together Ignore, Cancel Delete."**

The subconscious mind is only able to grasp specific trigger phrases; it is not able to understand conventional language.

These are known as "switch words," which are action or trigger words that communicate with the subconscious.

The Word's Power **TOGETHER**, indicates that our left and right brains work together to focus on and complete the task at hand. It also suggests that we focus on the task at hand as a group. Harmony is another meaning of it.

The superconscious mind is thought to be a higher plane of awareness that links people to universal truths, intuition, and their full potential. It is frequently linked to enlightenment, intense meditation, and peak experiences, in which people have a strong sense of insight, clarity, and a connection to something more than themselves. As I've already indicated, the alpha, theta, and delta states facilitate communication with our superconscious mind.

The superconscious mind, also known as your intuitive mind, it is only 20% strong, and in order to hear a message from your higher self, you must be well grounded and instill trust in what you hear.

Whenever you would encounter any challenges in your life your superconscious mind will alert you either through certain words that would come in your mind or through some written messages on hoarding or someone would give you some wise advice and so on, normally it is seen a normal individual tends to ignore these messages thinking it can be his own creation, It requires consistent trust on yourself in order to believe these downloads.

Techniques to release past Trauma or help overcome challenges

The Hidden Culprits: Unveiling the Emotional Roots of Unproductivity

Here is a small story which I wish to share

In a quaint village in northern India, lived a man named Mannu. Mannu, known to everyone as "The Dreamer," was always lost in visions of a beautiful, magnificent life. However, his dreams often led to anxiety and limiting beliefs, making every assigned task a source of immense stress. This lack of focus and positive mindset caused him to switch jobs frequently, unable to find his footing.

One day, a contractor approached Mannu with a golden opportunity. The contractor needed someone to supervise a team of labourers, a role that promised financial growth and potential promotions if executed well. Mannu, ever the dreamer, envisioned an easy path to success, seeing himself quickly rise to become the manager, then the top leader of the company.

Buoyed by confidence, zeal, and energy, Mannu eagerly accepted the job. However, upon arriving at the site, he was dismayed to find himself in a dusty construction area rather than an air-conditioned office. Feeling dejected, he voiced his concerns to the contractor, who reminded him that no such promises had been made. Determined to make the best of the situation, Mannu decided to stay and began meeting the labourers.

As Mannu connected with each labourer, he encountered a variety of mindsets and energy levels, which engulfed him in stress and anxiety. His dreams of a seamless ascent crumbled as he realized the complexity of managing diverse individuals with different realities and outlooks.

Feeling overwhelmed, Mannu returned home and confided in his elder brother, Sham. He shared his shattered dreams and the harsh reality he faced. Stressed and demotivated, Mannu feared catastrophic failure. Sham, with his calm demeanour, advised him to stay composed and focus on his work.

How many of you have faced similar situations, feeling challenged at your workplace, stressed, burned out, emotionally drained, and lacking motivation? We all yearn for a state of focused productivity at work, envisioning ourselves effortlessly tackling tasks, completing projects on time, and feeling a sense of accomplishment. Yet, the reality for many professionals is a constant battle against feelings of being frazzled and overwhelmed. Deadlines loom large, inboxes overflow, and a pervasive sense of low-grade stress hangs in the air. Surprisingly, this struggle with productivity often has an unexpected culprit: our emotions.

The Misunderstood Monster: Stress and the Fight-or-Flight Response

At the core of this issue lies the body's natural response to perceived threats – the **fight-or-flight response**. This primal survival mechanism, inherited from our ancestors, prepares us for immediate action when facing danger.

When encountering a hungry lion on the savannah, the surge of adrenaline and cortisol is crucial for survival – either to fight the threat or flee to safety.

However, in the modern workplace, the fight-or-flight response is often triggered by non-life-threatening situations – a looming deadline, a difficult conversation with a boss, or a public presentation. While the physiological response remains the same, the physical reaction is a mismatch – unnecessary and even detrimental in an office setting.

The constant activation of the fight-or-flight response due to chronic work stress creates a vicious cycle. Elevated heart rate, diverted blood flow, and hyper-arousal create a state of anxiety, difficulty focusing, and impaired memory. This stress hinders our ability to think critically, make sound decisions, and perform at our peak. Furthermore, chronic stress can negatively impact our physical well-being, leading to digestive issues namely acidity, liver issues, gall bladder issues, cause of diabetes and headaches, and even an increased risk of serious health problems like heart disease.

With our Character of this Book Mannu, when he saw the actual situation verses dream situation, he too had the similar feeling of fleeing, he was gripped with fear, stress and anxiety griped him

Beyond the Lion: Unveiling the Emotional Culprits

How many times have you been where you did not take the action due to underlying fears that triggered and stopped you from taking actions as you feared of falling down, or failing.

Similarly, the phrase "Beyond the Lion" metaphorically represents that an individual has his or her own fears and anxieties and the way an individual gets fearful to take any actions understanding the underlying emotional triggers that drive our fears and anxieties. Just as the lion symbolizes an immediate and tangible threat, our minds often create metaphorical lions—perceived dangers that trigger emotional responses. Unveiling these emotional culprits involves delving into the deeper psychological factors that shape our reactions and behaviour's. These recurring behaviours become into a personality

Identifying the Emotional Culprits

Types of Avoidance Behaviours

1. **Fear of Failure**: One of the most common emotional culprits is the fear of failure. This fear can paralyze individuals, preventing them from taking risks or pursuing their goals. It often stems from past experiences, perfectionism, or societal pressures. Understanding and addressing this fear can help individuals build resilience and confidence.

2. **Fear of Rejection**: The fear of rejection is another significant emotional trigger. It can lead to avoidance behaviours, social anxiety, and a reluctance to express oneself fully. This fear is often rooted in a desire for acceptance and validation from others. Unveiling this culprit involves recognizing the value of self-acceptance and building self-esteem.

3. **Perfectionism**: Perfectionism is the need to meet exceptionally high standards, often to the detriment of one's well-being. It can lead to chronic stress, procrastination, and dissatisfaction. Perfectionism

creates fear of failure, it is essential to begin and make changes as you walk the path. Understanding that perfection is an unrealistic and unattainable goal can help individuals focus on progress and self-improvement rather than flawlessness. It is always better to Start Simple Sooner instead of trying to procrastination.

4. **Past Trauma**: Traumatic experiences can leave deep emotional scars that influence current behaviour's and reactions. Trauma can manifest as heightened anxiety, avoidance, and hypervigilance. Addressing past trauma through hypno-therapy and self-care is crucial for healing and moving forward.

5. **Low Self-Esteem**: Low self-esteem can significantly impact how individuals perceive and respond to challenges. It can lead to self-doubt, negative self-talk, and a lack of confidence. Building self-esteem involves recognizing and challenging negative beliefs about oneself and celebrating personal strengths and achievements.

6. **Unresolved Grief**: Many a times an individual might have undergone Social comparisons in his childhood or even at his workplace that would create Unresolved grief from past as a result creating anxiety, depression, and difficulty moving forward. Acknowledging and processing grief through counselling, support groups, or personal reflection is essential for emotional healing.

The fight-or-flight response is just one piece of the puzzle. Unveiling the emotional roots of unproductivity involves delving deeper into the subtle ways our emotions sabotage our best intentions. Here are some key culprits:

Negative Thought Patterns: Our internal dialogue or self-talk plays a significant role in shaping our emotional state and this is programmed based on how your childhood has been or how emotionally you were attacked and how withdrawn have you been. Many professionals fall prey to negative thought patterns like

Catastrophizing relates to a distorted mind where an individual irrationally assumes the worst possible outcome of a situation, this often happens when their anxiety and stress amplifies. In this state the person starts imagining and expecting disastrous results without any real basis for such conclusions.

For Example, when an individual commits a minor mistake at work, he may believe that he would be fired, become unemployed, and face financial ruin. This mental habit not only increases emotional distress but can also lead to avoidance behaviours, this further can also affect the liver too.

Avoidance behaviours are actions taken to escape or prevent situations that cause anxiety, fear, or discomfort. These behaviours are a common response to distress and are often associated with anxiety disorders, such as generalized anxiety disorder (GAD), social anxiety disorder, and post-traumatic stress disorder (PTSD). While avoidance might provide temporary relief, it can reinforce and perpetuate anxiety in the long run, leading to a cycle of avoidance and increased fear. Some individuals can turn towards addiction

Types of Avoidance Behaviours

1. **Situational Avoidance**: This involves steering clear of specific situations that trigger anxiety. For instance, someone with social anxiety may avoid parties, meetings, or public speaking events to prevent feelings of embarrassment or judgment.

2. **Cognitive Avoidance**: This occurs when individuals distract themselves from distressing thoughts or emotions. They might engage in excessive TV watching, internet browsing, or other activities to avoid dealing with their anxious thoughts.

3. **Safety Behaviours**: These are actions taken to feel safe or reduce perceived danger in an anxiety-provoking situation. Example, always carrying medication for panic attacks or only attending events with a trusted friend.

4. **Substance Use**: Some individuals turn to alcohol, drugs, or medication to numb their anxiety or escape from stressful situations.

Individuals with Avoidance habit generally fail in networking and can lead to loss of opportunity.

Procrastination: Here I again explain about procrastination. Delaying or putting off tasks that cause anxiety, such as completing work assignments, making important decisions, or confronting difficult conversations, is another form of avoidance. It is also found that people who are perfectionist tend to procrastinate and create delays which leads to stress and anxiety.

It is said that Procrastination invites delays and further attracts loss of opportunity which further creates poverty

Procrastination is the act of delaying or postponing tasks or decisions, often to the detriment of one's productivity and well-being. It is a common behaviour that can affect anyone, regardless of age, occupation, or personal circumstances. Procrastination often involves putting off tasks that are perceived as difficult, unpleasant, or intimidating, in favour of more enjoyable or less challenging activities.

Causes of Procrastination

1. Perfectionism:

Perfectionism is an avoidance tactic. It promises us that if we use it, we will avoid feeling negative emotions, stressed, rejection from others and feeling of failure, The answer is it doesn't work

Have you seen some individuals who want everything very perfect, ideally it is said perfectionist are time wasters as they do not start any task The desire to complete tasks perfectly can lead to procrastination. Individuals may delay starting or finishing a task because they fear it won't meet their high standards.

Fear of Failure:

"You can't let your failures define you. You have to let your failures teach you." — Barack Obama

Anxiety about not succeeding or making mistakes can cause people to avoid tasks altogether. The fear of negative outcomes can be paralyzing and lead to chronic procrastination.

Let me give you an example through a story of Manu, In the village where Manu lived there was river and on the other side of the river there was a village which was situated on a hill, there was a wooden bridge that connected both the villages, during Monsoon one day there were huge rains due to which the river started to overflow and Manu's village started to flood, the situation was so greave some that people's houses were damaged more importantly the bridge that connected the village was damaged and broken

Sham was a man who always looked for solutions even in crisis, he told Manu that both of them need to go to a tree near the river whose branch was very big and almost touched the other part of the river, Sham asked Manu to immediately start walking along with him, however Manu was gripped with fear and did not move a inch, Sham later left him and started walking in the flooded water towards the tree, in some time after battling the floods he reached the tree and managed to climb the tree. He waited for Manu so that together they could go to the other side of the river, however Manu did not show up and eventually Sham started slowing crawling on the branch of the tree and eventually he reached the other side of the river, On reaching Sham kept on shouting for Manu however his voice did not reach Manu.

This story teaches us to be in awareness and take right decision instead of not taking any actions due to fear.

2. Lack of Motivation:

"Opportunity is missed by most people because it is dressed in overalls and looks like work."
-Thomas Edison

When tasks are seen as boring or irrelevant, individuals may struggle to find the motivation to begin or complete them. There can be past failures which might have impacted the individuals emotionally and that can lead to lack of motivation which further leads to procrastination

In the above story Manu was fearful of the situation and did not take the required steps to reach a safe place and struggled in the flooded waters, individuals do not take required steps when they are in the phase of anxiety or stress, it is essential to seek help from a coach or seeking help from their leaders, the core reasons from their anxiety can further impact the entire personality of a person in a negative manner.

3. Poor Time Management:

"Concentrate all your thoughts upon the work in hand. The sun's rays do not burn until brought to a focus."
- Alexander Graham Bell

Difficulty in prioritizing tasks and managing time effectively can result in procrastination. Without a clear plan, it's easy to become overwhelmed and put off important tasks.

4. **Task Aversion**: Tasks that are perceived as unpleasant, tedious, or overwhelming are often procrastinated. Whenever there is lack of process

individuals may avoid starting such tasks to escape the discomfort associated with them.

5. **Distractions**: The presence of distractions, such as social media, television, or other entertainment, can lead individuals to procrastinate. These distractions provide immediate gratification, which is more appealing than the effort required for the task at hand.

Effects of Procrastination

1. **Decreased Productivity**: Procrastination often leads to last-minute rushes to complete tasks, which can result in lower quality work and missed deadlines.

2. **Increased Stress and Anxiety**: As deadlines approach and tasks remain incomplete, stress and anxiety levels can rise, creating a cycle of procrastination and stress.

3. **Negative Impact on Relationships**: Chronic procrastination can strain relationships with colleagues, supervisors, and loved ones who may rely on timely completion of tasks.

4. **Lowered Self-Esteem**: Repeated procrastination can lead to feelings of guilt, shame, and inadequacy, which can negatively impact self-esteem and confidence.

5. **Health Consequences**: The stress and anxiety associated with procrastination can contribute to physical health issues, such as headaches, insomnia, and weakened immune function.

The root of catastrophizing often lies in underlying anxiety or past traumatic experiences that skew one's perception of reality. Cognitive-behavioural therapy is a common treatment approach, in this treatment the individual is made to focus on present day situation instead of past situations, helping individuals recognize and challenge these irrational thoughts, and gradually replace them with more balanced and realistic thinking patterns. By addressing the cognitive distortions that fuel catastrophizing, individuals can reduce their anxiety and improve their overall well-being.

Developing mindfulness and stress management techniques can also be beneficial. Practices such as meditation, deep breathing exercises, and journaling can help individuals stay grounded in the present moment, reducing the tendency to spiral into catastrophic thinking. Ultimately, overcoming catastrophizing requires patience and consistent effort, but it is achievable with the right support and strategies.

Overgeneralizing - is a cognitive distortion where individuals make broad and sweeping statements based on limited evidence, it involves applying specific observations or experiences to an entire category or situation, often leading to inaccurate or skewed perceptions.

For example, if someone has a negative experience with one colleague, they might overgeneralize by assuming that all colleagues will behave similarly. This thinking pattern can limit personal growth and damage relationships, as it prevents individuals from seeing situations and people as unique.

1. **Mental filtering:** These distorted thoughts fuel anxiety and create a sense of helplessness, hindering our motivation and productivity. Individuals focus exclusively on the negative aspects of a situation while ignoring or dismissing any positive elements. This selective attention to unfavourable details creates a skewed perception of reality, often leading to increased stress and a pessimistic outlook. For instance, if someone receives a performance review with both positive feedback and constructive criticism, they might fixate only on the negative comments, overlooking the praise they received.

2. **Limiting Beliefs:** Deep-seated limiting beliefs like "I'm not good enough" or "I can't handle this workload" can severely restrict our potential. These beliefs, often formed in childhood or past experiences, hold us back from taking risks, learning new things, and challenging ourselves.

3. **The Perfectionism Trap:** The relentless pursuit of perfection can be a major productivity killer. Striving to meet unrealistic expectations leads to anxiety, procrastination, and a fear of failure. This perfectionist mindset can paralyze us, preventing us from taking the first step and making progress.

4. **Emotional Triggers:** We all have unique situations or personality traits that trigger strong emotional responses. For some, it might be public speaking, tight deadlines, or micromanagement. Understanding

these triggers and their emotional impact is crucial for managing them effectively.

5. **Work-Life Imbalance:** When our personal and professional lives are constantly out of sync, it can lead to feelings of stress, exhaustion, and resentment. This lack of balance spills over into our work performance, affecting our focus, motivation, and creativity.

The whispers in Your Head: Identifying Negative Thought Patterns and Limiting Beliefs

We have visited about self-talk, have you ever sat down to tackle a task, only to find yourself bombarded by a barrage of negative self-talk? A voice whispers doubts, criticizes your abilities, and magnifies potential failures, are the embodiment of negative thought patterns and limiting beliefs that can significantly hinder your productivity and overall well-being.

This chapter equips you to identify these patterns of self-talk and limiting beliefs and challenge their hold on your thinking. By recognizing these patterns and reframing them with a more empowering mindset, you can unlock your true potential and approach work with greater confidence and focus.

Discovering the Power of Positive Self-Talk

In 1999, I was working in a multinational organization and had a challenging daily commute, traveling by local bus for about an hour and a half. Each morning, I left home stressed, convinced I would be late to the office. Unsurprisingly, I often arrived late.

A Transformative Discovery

In 2000, I came across Rhonda Byrne's book, "The Secret." For the first time, I understood how our internal dialogue creates challenges. The book emphasized that the universe doesn't understand words like "don't," "no," and "not." Intrigued, I decided to change my internal dialogue. Instead of stressing about being late, I began affirming, "I will reach the office by 8:45 am." To my amazement, I started arriving on time. The universe was aligning everything according to my positive affirmations.

Implementing Affirmations

Thrilled and excited by this discovery, I made a conscious effort to use simple affirmative sentences and set a filter for my thoughts. Initially, this was a draining activity, requiring constant awareness, but the benefits were undeniable.

The Impact of Internal Dialogue

Our internal dialogue, the constant stream of thoughts running through our minds, plays a crucial role in shaping our emotional state and influencing our actions. Positive self-talk can be a powerful motivator, boosting our confidence and resilience. On the other hand, negative self-talk, characterized by distorted thinking patterns, can significantly drain our energy and motivation.

Influence of Others Narratives

It's also important to recognize how easily we get connected to other people's narratives on any subject, starting to believe and attach to those narratives. When we believe someone else's narrative, we give consent to the universe to begin creating similar realities for ourselves.

For instance, during the COVID-19 pandemic, the media was saturated with negative news about the rising number of deaths, causing widespread panic. I consciously chose not to absorb this fear. Whenever I encountered negative news, I would affirm, "I am safe, secure, and well-guarded. Thank you, Divine, for your grace over me and my family." I never agreed with the fearful narratives being communicated by the media or individuals. While my neighbours were very fearful and three out of four family members were diagnosed with COVID, my family and I remained safe.

The Power of Faith Over Fear

Fear can be incredibly damaging. Here's a story about a worker named John to illustrate this point:

The Story of John

In 1999, John was a cold storage supervisor in Texas. One day, after completing his quality check, he was noting down observations and preparing to restart the cold storage machines. Unbeknownst to John, a security guard, thinking the room was empty, closed and locked the main exit door from the outside.

Panic and Fear

John, realizing he was trapped, began shouting and banging on the door for help, but no one could hear him. Gripped by fear, he started trembling, convinced that if help didn't arrive within 30 minutes, he would surely die. Half an hour passed, and John started shivering, feeling his body going numb. He fell to the floor, slowly losing consciousness, and eventually died within a few hours.

The Discovery

The next day, an employee opened the cold storage and found John's body. The senior staff called a doctor, who declared John dead due to freezing. Shocked, the employees informed the doctor that the cold storage was undergoing maintenance, and all the machines were off. The temperature in the room was normal, so how could John have frozen to death?

The Investigation

A team of central bureau officers conducted an investigation and concluded that John died because he believed the cold storage was operational. His brain sent signals to his body, creating a perception of severe cold. This psychological state led his body to react as if it were freezing, ultimately causing his death.

The Lesson

Had John remembered that the machines were off and the room temperature was normal, he could have saved his life. This story illustrates the profound impact of our thoughts and beliefs on our physical reality. Fear and judgments can create immense harm, leading us to take drastic actions based on perceived threats rather than actual dangers.

Overcoming Fear and Negative Beliefs

It's crucial to ground ourselves in reality and seek guidance when facing challenging situations. Often, individuals avoid discussing their fears and challenges, fearing judgment from others. However, sharing our struggles and seeking help can provide new perspectives and solutions.

Practical Techniques

When your mind starts to chatter with limiting or threatening beliefs, use powerful switch words like "SHUT UP AND GET LOST" or "SHUT UP and FORGET." Repeatedly chanting these phrases for two to three minutes as negative thoughts appear can help shift your energy levels and mindset.

Real-Life Application

In my own experience, while working in one of my organizations, senior management would often assign ambitious targets. When asked if we could achieve them, I always responded positively, saying, "Yes, we will do it." Despite my sales team expressing concerns about market conditions, I maintained that it was their belief system creating barriers. By focusing on the desired numbers and aligning tasks accordingly, we often met and even exceeded our targets.

The Importance of Mindset

Starting any task with a negative mindset creates emotional blockages that lead to procrastination. Procrastination is a thief of time, often driven by fear of failure or the belief that perfection must be attained before beginning. However, perfection is achieved through continuous effort and learning from imperfections.

Commitment, Focus, and Timeliness (CFT)

Commitment, Focus, and Timeliness are essential components for achieving goals. Failing to adhere to these principles leads to missed opportunities. Embrace failures as stepping stones to success, learning from mistakes rather than blaming others.

Embracing Imperfection

Human beings are imperfect, and we are here to learn. Successful people have also faced failures, learned from them, and paved their path to success. Earth is considered the toughest school in the universe, and the lessons we learn prevent repeated patterns in our lives. Ignoring these lessons makes them increasingly difficult.

It is essential that Our internal dialogue and belief systems shape our reality. By maintaining positive self-talk, rejecting negative narratives, and focusing on solutions, we can align ourselves with the abundance and opportunities the universe offers. Embrace your imperfections, learn from your experiences, and trust in your ability to shape a better future.

Common Culprits: Unveiling Negative Thought Patterns

Here are some of the most common negative thought patterns that plague working professionals:

- **Catastrophizing:** this involves blowing situations out of proportion and assuming the worst possible outcome. ("If I miss this deadline, I'm sure I'll get fired!")

- **Overgeneralizing:** Making broad negative conclusions based on a single event. ("I messed up this presentation, I'm obviously a failure at everything!")

- **Mental Filtering:** Focusing solely on the negative aspects of a situation while ignoring the positives. ("They only noticed the typos in my report, not all the hard work I put in.")

- **Discounting the Positive:** Downplaying or dismissing positive experiences or compliments. ("My boss said my work was good, but they were probably just being nice.")

- **Emotional Reasoning:** Believing that your emotions accurately reflect reality. ("I feel overwhelmed, so I must be incapable of handling this project.")

These negative thought patterns create a distorted perception of reality, fuelling anxiety, self-doubt, and hindering your ability to approach challenges constructively.

Limiting Beliefs: The Invisible Barriers

Beyond negative thought patterns, limiting beliefs act as invisible barriers restricting your potential. These are core beliefs often formed in childhood or through past experiences that shape how you see yourself and your capabilities. Examples include:

- "I'm not good enough."
- "I can't handle pressure."
- "I'm not a creative person."
- "I'm not smart enough to succeed in this field."

Parents hold very important role in forming belief systems, It is important for every parent to ensure negative belief systems should not be planted in their children.

One of my client believed he was not special and no one loved him, during the self-hypnosis session he was constantly seeing cake, candles and balloons, when he was asked what did this indicate to him, he mentioned that his parents even though they were in good financial condition did not celebrate his birthday, whenever he was invited to his friends birthday he felt he was not loved and felt ignored, when we did certain emotional healing sessions he was able to overcome 60% from this situation.

It is important to note that healing is a gradual process and no magic happens overnight, it requires consistent efforts to clear all the emotional clutter that we have tamed in the subconscious mind.

Limiting beliefs hold you back from taking risks, learning new skills, and stepping outside your comfort zone. They create a sense of helplessness and can lead to procrastination and avoidance of challenging tasks.

In order to get answers for any situations that you feel stuck or you need any guidance start asking questions which will have the word "Would"

I see word **"Would"** as a Possibility word and whenever we ask questions that begin with the below statements you ask the subconscious mind to look in the universe and get answers

The questions can begin with

What would it take for me to excel in this work

What is stopping me from creating

What is it that is creating illness or ill health

What is it that I am not acknowledging

Strategies for Change

The good news is that you are not at the mercy of your thoughts and beliefs. Here are some strategies to identify and challenge these negative patterns:

- **Catch Yourself in the Act:** Pay attention to your internal dialogue. When you notice negative self-talk, acknowledge it without judgment.

  For Example when I was practising to filter my thoughts after I read "The Secret" and whenever I used to slip into castle of thoughts and would be trapped in, and when I would catch myself in the act of self talk I would try to reverse the entire thoughts go to the root and understand what got me into this castle of thoughts, here I was able to understand which person or image or certain words triggered me, so this would help me understand on what I had to work and heal accordingly. I would say the below affirmation

"Whatever is creating this thought pattern I dissolve it completely from its source and my entire existence of my reality coming from any time space and dimension, I set myself free from this event now, I am healed I am free, I am free I am free Now"

This above affirmation needs to be said consciously each time you encounter such self-talk situations.

- **Question the Validity:** Ask yourself if your thoughts are based on reality or distorted perceptions. Are there any alternative explanations for the situation?
- **Challenge the thoughts:** Once you identify a negative thought pattern, actively challenge its validity. Would you speak to a friend this way?

Journaling for Self-Discovery:

Journaling is a powerful tool for self-awareness and transformation. Regularly write down your thoughts and feelings, paying attention to recurring negative patterns. Over time, journaling can help you identify your gremlins and develop strategies to challenge them.

Building a Growth Mindset:

Shifting from a fixed mindset ("I am what I am") to a growth mindset ("I can learn and grow") is crucial for overcoming limiting beliefs. Embrace challenges as opportunities to learn and develop new skills.

I introduce here a method called **RECHARGE**

In order to build yourself to a Growth Mindset it is important for you to adopt this RECHARGE method, a journey towards your identity

RE - Rebrand yourself

C - Confident Communication

H - Handle complex Situations

A - Appreciate

R - Resilience

G - Generate Opportunity

E - Elevate

Rebranding Yourself: A Journey of Identity

Rebranding yourself isn't just about changing your resume or updating your LinkedIn profile. It's a deep dive into your identity, values, and aspirations. Here's a roadmap to guide you through this transformative journey:

1. Self-Discovery and Reflection:

- In order to rebrand yourself you need to deep dive in identifying where you wish to see yourself (your

Goals), and what is your current state, what are your current value drivers and what value drivers would you need to inculcate in order to reach your goals.

- Analyse Your Current Brand: How are you currently perceived by colleagues and potential employers? Take a look at your online presence (LinkedIn, social media) and offline interactions. Does this reflect your desired brand?

- How would you like see yourself in coming six to twelve months define it accordingly, this has to be from your thought level to your manifestation of what you want to be, what changes you need to do whether on financial, health, knowledge etc

- **Identify Your Core Values:** What truly matters to you? What are your guiding principles?

- **Discover Your Strengths and Passions:** What are you naturally good at? What energizes you?

- Here I wish to tell you that whichever job you are in you need to introspect if this is your passion and are you obsessed with your work, Do you love your work or does your work trouble you in the sense does it create stress on you. This is the first level of analysis that you need to do.

Understand Your Weaknesses:

- What areas do you need to improve or delegate? Here I would recommend you seek help from your seniors and also your family members as you will get unfiltered inputs. We are normally not willing to look at our weaknesses until we are under any improvement plan or you are put in a coaching session. Be true to yourself, the difference between the top successful individuals and average person is the lack of commitment.

Crafting Your Personal Narrative:

- **Develop a Compelling Story:** Your personal narrative is the story you tell about yourself. It should be authentic, inspiring, and memorable. Define smaller versions of yourself which will be measurable, for example if you are a wake up in late hours or go to bed late make sure you make a change in this schedule, as the saying goes, "Early to bed, early to rise makes a man health wealthy and wise"

  Reduce your time over gadgets and mobile, stop scrolling you are feeding the dopamine which will slow you down and will make you lazy instead be more active, approach your phone only while needed. Make every effort to see to it that you remain focused and not distracted

- **Highlight Your Unique Selling Proposition (USP):** What sets you apart from others in your field?
- **Align Your Brand with Your Goals:** Ensure your personal brand supports your career aspirations and long-term goals.

Cultivating Your Online Presence:

- **Optimize Your LinkedIn Profile:** Showcase your expertise, skills, and accomplishments. Use keywords effectively.
- **Build a Personal Website or Blog:** Share your knowledge, insights, and personality.
- **Leverage Social Media:** Choose platforms that align with your target audience and consistently share valuable content.
- **Create a Strong Personal Brand Identity:** Develop a consistent visual identity across all platforms.

Networking and Relationship Building:

- **Expand Your Network:** Connect with people in your industry and beyond.
- **Attend Industry Events:** Network with potential employers, clients, and collaborators.
- **Leverage Online Communities:** Participate in online forums and groups related to your field.
- **Build Strong Relationships:** Focus on quality over quantity.

Continuous Learning and Growth:

- **Stay Updated:** Keep abreast of industry trends and developments.
- **Acquire New Skills:** Develop new skills to enhance your value proposition.

- **Seek Mentorship:** Learn from experienced professionals.
- **Embrace Feedback:** Use feedback to improve and grow.

Authenticity and Consistency:
- **Be Genuine:** Authenticity is key to building trust and credibility.
- **Practice Consistency:** Ensure your actions align with your personal brand.
- **Stay True to Your Values:** Your values should be the foundation of your rebranding efforts.
- **Keep a Tracker:** have a start and end date, you need to be very committed to your transformation and need to put tiny efforts in order to see the bigger change in you

Remember: Rebranding is a journey, not a destination. It requires continuous effort and adaptation. Be patient with yourself, celebrate small wins, and most importantly, enjoy the process of becoming the best version of yourself.

The path to the Top is lonely

This is such an important fact as once people around you will see that you are now serious about your growth they can tend to break your confidence, these can be your friends your relatives or even your acquaintances. Some friends can just walk away or ignore you; this indicates that you are doing excellent and you need to focus on path to your success. You need to abide some rules

Rule no 1 – Never disclose your Goals to anyone expecting your Coach if you have one or to your nearest person whom you have faith in.

Rule no 2 – Make sure that you are very punctual and work on growth mindset

Rule no 3 – You will have to work on your inner habits, it might be that the individual drives confidence issues and also self-trust. 80% mindset plays a vital role, here mindset is not only about work, it also speaks about how you portray yourself internally and externally, how are you able to exhibit yourself to other, how are you placed in terms of receiving.

Receiving or Self Worth - When Receiving is the key blockage, i.e., the person has challenges to demand in his work, like asking a raise or asking for payment or money, asking for promotion, the individual feels blocked to ask and may tend to lose on this aspect, it is essential that the individual needs to fix this and this can be done by healing your stress or past trauma that must have got you here. A healer or a coach can help you in this regard.

To understand what Self-Worth is, It's like believing that you don't deserve happiness, success, or love. It's feeling unsure of yourself and your abilities. It's like thinking your opinions don't matter and that you're not important. You have challenges to ask for a raise or even to take your money for the efforts made.

An individual with lack of self-worth can majorly tend to be in anxious and state of fear. Imagine looking in a mirror and not recognizing the person looking back. That's what it feels like to lack self-worth. It's a sense of emptiness and unworthiness.

Hence, it's essential to carve your own path, there are certain principles that can guide you towards success while maintaining your integrity and fostering positive relationships.

The internal Communication is key for succeeding

Communication – Begins with self, if the communication is fear or anxious based the external communication too will indicate the same. Key parameters to work on communication are

Cultivate a Growth Mindset

- **Embrace Challenges:** View obstacles as opportunities for growth and learning.
- **Learn from Failures:** See setbacks as valuable lessons, not personal defeats.
- **Seek Feedback:** Actively solicit feedback to identify areas for improvement.
- **Continuous Learning:** Stay curious and committed to lifelong learning.

Build Strong Relationships

- **Authenticity:** Be genuine in your interactions with self and others and build trust with yourself and others.

- **Empathy:** Understand and share the feelings of others.
- **Collaboration:** Foster teamwork and collaboration to achieve shared goals.
- **Mentorship:** Seek guidance from experienced professionals like coaches or mentor or anyone whom you look upon whenever you need one.

Develop Exceptional Leadership Skills

- **Visionary Thinking:** Develop a clear and inspiring vision for the future. Example do not just say I want to earn 5 crore Rupees by end of 2028, you will have to have a step-by-step process on how are you going to achieve it and what actions would be required, each step has to be time bound.
- **Emotional Intelligence:** Understand and manage your own emotions and those of others. Communication with self is important, make sure you positive affirmative words with self, never ever say to yourself as a joke that you are a looser, people always treat you in this way.

    Your emotional intelligence will only improve if you trust and treat yourself with respect, your body and mind are vessel in this life do not exploit them by negative self-talk.

- **Decision-Making:** Make informed and timely decisions with confidence.

- **Delegation:** Empower others by delegating tasks and responsibilities.
- **Learn to Say No:** If you find it challenging to do a job that is assigned to you gently say no or assign the work if you are a leader to your team member who is good at the job
- **Eliminate Delegate and Consolidate** – Use this technique to be focused on your work, eliminate all the unwanted documents from your table, Delegate the work who will do much efficiently and quickly and consolidate, which means prioritise the work which needs to be done the next day, you can create a tray or a file which will help you to work faster
- **Use the Eisenhower decision matrix** – if you have too many activities to do and are unable to decide which should be done then use the Eisenhower technique that will help you focus on prioritising your activity

Maintain Integrity and Ethics

- **Honesty and Transparency:** Build trust through open and honest communication.
- **Ethical Decision-Making:** Make choices that align with your values and organizational principles.
- **Accountability:** Take responsibility for your actions and their consequences.

- **Professionalism:** Uphold high standards of conduct and behaviour.

Prioritize Self-Care

- **Work-Life Balance:** Set boundaries between work and personal life.
- **Physical Health:** Prioritize exercise, nutrition, and sleep.
- **Mental Well-being:** Practice mindfulness, meditation, or other stress management techniques.
- **Continuous Learning:** Invest in personal growth and development.

Embrace Challenges and Risks

- **Step Outside Your Comfort Zone:** Embrace opportunities for growth and development.
- **Calculated Risks:** Take calculated risks to achieve your goals.
- **Resilience:** Develop the ability to bounce back from setbacks.

Handling Complex situations comes with stronger Self worth and strong communication skills, the person can get work done if these two parameters are strong in his personality

Any kind of challenging situation can be dealt when one knows his or her capability to resolve complex situations, Technology can always change but an individual's perspective towards getting things done varies based on how confident and worthy he or she feel internally.

One cannot fake self-worth as his actions will be seen it is crucial for an individual to dive into his personality and check how he or she resonates as an individual.

1. Handling Complex Situations

Whenever an individual gets stressed of any complex situations and gets into anxious mode, the individual activates the below and working on these triggers is key.

Stress and Anxiety Activation

- **Fight-or-Flight Response**: When stress or anxiety is triggered, the body activates the sympathetic nervous system. This leads to the release of stress hormones like adrenaline and cortisol. This response prepares the body to either confront or flee from the threat.

- **Symptoms**: This stage is characterized by physiological changes such as increased heart rate, rapid breathing, heightened blood pressure, and a burst of energy. While beneficial in short-term situations, chronic activation can lead to detrimental health effects.

2. Neurological Impact

Central Nervous System

- **Brain Function**: Chronic stress affects brain structure and function. The prefrontal cortex, which governs executive functions like decision-making, attention, and working memory, can shrink with prolonged exposure to stress. Conversely, the amygdala, which processes emotions like fear and anxiety, can become more reactive.

- **Symptoms**: Cognitive impairments such as memory problems, difficulties in concentrating, decision-making challenges, and an increased risk of developing anxiety disorders and depression are common.

3. **Cardiovascular System**

Heart and Blood Vessels

- **Increased Heart Rate and Blood Pressure**: Persistent stress causes the heart to work harder and blood vessels to constrict, leading to consistently high blood pressure.
- **Symptoms**: Over time, this can result in hypertension, increasing the risk of heart attacks, strokes, and other cardiovascular diseases.

4. **Respiratory System**

Breathing Patterns

- **Rapid Breathing**: Stress often leads to shallow, rapid breathing, known as hyperventilation, which can decrease carbon dioxide levels in the blood.
- **Symptoms**: This can cause dizziness, light-headedness, and can trigger panic attacks.

Chronic stress can exacerbate respiratory conditions like asthma and lead to shortness of breath.

5. Gastrointestinal System

Digestive Health

- **Digestive Disorders**: Stress affects the digestive tract, disrupting normal digestive processes. The body may produce excess stomach acid, slow down or speed up the movement of food through the intestines, and alter gut microbiota balance.
- **Symptoms**: This can lead to conditions such as irritable bowel syndrome (IBS), acid reflux, gastritis, ulcers, and changes in appetite (overeating or loss of appetite), causing weight fluctuations and gastrointestinal discomfort.

6. Musculoskeletal System

Muscle Tension

- **Muscle Contractions**: Chronic stress causes muscles to remain in a constant state of guardedness, leading to tension and muscle spasms.
- **Symptoms**: This manifests as headaches, migraines, and chronic pain, particularly in the neck, shoulders, and back. Long-term muscle tension can contribute to musculoskeletal disorders.

7. Endocrine System

Hormonal Imbalance

- **Cortisol Production**: Prolonged stress leads to sustained high levels of cortisol, which can disrupt various bodily functions.
- **Symptoms**: High cortisol levels can cause weight gain, particularly around the abdomen, increase the risk of diabetes, contribute to fatigue, and disrupt sleep patterns, leading to insomnia or poor-quality sleep.

8. Immune System

- **Weakened Immune Response**: Chronic stress suppresses the immune system, making the body less effective at fighting off infections and more susceptible to illnesses.
- **Symptoms**: This results in an increased frequency of colds, infections, and slower recovery times from illnesses and injuries. Stress can also exacerbate autoimmune conditions.

9. Reproductive System

Sexual Health

- **Hormonal Disruptions**: Stress affects the production of reproductive hormones like estrogen, progesterone, and testosterone.
- **Symptoms**: For women, this can lead to menstrual irregularities, premenstrual syndrome (PMS), and exacerbation of menopausal

symptoms. For men, it can cause reduced libido and erectile dysfunction. Both genders may experience reduced fertility.

10. Skin and Hair

Dermatological Issues

- **Skin Conditions**: Stress can trigger or worsen skin conditions such as acne, eczema, and psoriasis due to the inflammatory response it induces.

- **Hair Loss**: Chronic stress can disrupt the hair growth cycle, leading to conditions like telogen effluvium, where hair falls out more easily.

- **Symptoms**: Breakouts, rashes, and noticeable hair thinning or loss are common. Stress can also cause skin to become more sensitive and reactive.

The Emotional Roots of Physical Ailments: Unveiling the Mind-Body Connection

In the realm of holistic health, it is increasingly acknowledged that our emotions play a significant role in shaping our physical well-being. The intricate interplay between our mind and body means that unresolved emotional issues can manifest as physical ailments. Understanding these emotional roots can be pivotal in addressing and healing various health challenges. Let's delve into the emotional reasons behind common health issues such as digestive disorders, breathing difficulties, immune system problems, weaker muscles and bones, and eyesight issues.

Digestive Issues: The Emotional Gut Connection

The digestive system, often referred to as the "second brain," is highly sensitive to our emotional state. Emotional stress and unresolved trauma can wreak havoc on our gut health, leading to conditions such as irritable bowel syndrome (IBS), acid reflux, and ulcers.

1. **Stress and Anxiety**: Chronic stress triggers the release of cortisol and adrenaline, which can disrupt the balance of gut bacteria and lead to inflammation. Anxiety can also cause the digestive system to become hypersensitive, resulting in symptoms like bloating, cramps, and diarrhea.

2. **Suppressed Emotions**: Emotions such as anger, fear, and sadness that are not expressed or processed can be stored in the digestive system. This can manifest as physical tension and discomfort, leading to conditions like constipation or irritable bowel syndrome.

3. **Fear of Change**: The gut is often associated with our ability to "digest" life's experiences. A fear of change or difficulty in processing life events can cause digestive disturbances, reflecting an emotional struggle to assimilate new experiences.

Breathing Difficulties: The Breath of Emotions

Our respiratory system is intimately linked with our emotional state. Breathing difficulties, such as asthma and chronic bronchitis, often have emotional underpinnings.

1. **Anxiety and Panic**: Anxiety often manifests through rapid, shallow breathing or hyperventilation. Panic

attacks can cause a feeling of suffocation, tightening the chest, and making it hard to breathe.

2. **Grief and Sadness**: The lungs are associated with grief and sadness in many traditional healing systems. Unresolved grief can lead to chronic respiratory problems, reflecting a metaphorical difficulty in "letting go."

3. **Suppression of Expression**: Holding back from expressing emotions, particularly anger and frustration, can cause tension in the respiratory muscles, leading to breathing difficulties.

Immune System Issues: The Emotional Shield

The immune system is our body's defence mechanism, and its functionality is deeply affected by our emotional health. Emotional stress can weaken the immune system, making us more susceptible to infections and autoimmune diseases.

1. **Chronic Stress**: Prolonged exposure to stress hormones like cortisol can suppress the immune response, reducing the body's ability to fight off infections and heal wounds.

2. **Emotional Trauma**: Past emotional traumas can lead to chronic inflammation and autoimmune disorders. The body may turn against itself, reflecting internal conflicts and unresolved emotional pain.

3. **Lack of Boundaries**: Inability to establish healthy emotional boundaries can lead to overburdening the

immune system. This can manifest as frequent colds, allergies, and other immune-related conditions.

Weaker Muscles and Bones: The Emotional Foundation

Our musculoskeletal system provides the framework for our physical body, and its strength is influenced by our emotional state. Emotional stress can lead to muscle tension, weakness, and bone-related issues.

1. **Chronic Stress and Tension**: Persistent emotional stress causes the muscles to remain in a constant state of tension, leading to chronic pain, stiffness, and weakness. This can also affect bone health, as tension can alter posture and alignment, causing wear and tear on the skeletal system.

2. **Lack of Support**: Feelings of insecurity and lack of emotional support can manifest as weakened muscles and brittle bones. The body reflects the mind's struggle to "stand strong" and maintain stability in the face of emotional challenges.

3. **Suppressed Anger and Frustration**: Suppressed anger can lead to tightness and rigidity in the muscles, while long-term frustration can weaken the musculoskeletal system, making it more susceptible to injuries and conditions like osteoporosis.

Eyesight Issues: The Emotional Vision

Our eyes are not only the windows to the world but also to our inner emotional state. Emotional factors can significantly influence vision problems such as myopia, hyperopia, and even more severe conditions.

1. **Fear of the Future**: Myopia (near-sightedness) is often linked to a fear of what lies ahead. Individuals with unresolved anxieties about the future may struggle to see things clearly at a distance.

2. **Difficulty in Seeing the Present**: Hyperopia (farsightedness) can be associated with a reluctance to deal with current issues. Avoidance of present emotional challenges can blur our ability to focus on the here and now.

3. **Emotional Overload**: Stress and emotional overload can lead to eye strain and tension, causing headaches and visual disturbances. The eyes reflect our mind's struggle to process and "see" through the overwhelming emotions.

Conclusion: Healing Through Emotional Awareness

Understanding the emotional roots of physical ailments empowers us to address the underlying causes rather than just treating the symptoms. By acknowledging and processing our emotions, we can initiate profound healing that transcends the physical plane.

1. **Mindfulness and Meditation**: Practices that promote mindfulness and meditation can help in identifying and releasing suppressed emotions, reducing stress, and restoring balance to the body's systems.

2. **Emotional Expression**: Encouraging healthy emotional expression through journaling, therapy, or

creative outlets can prevent emotional suppression and its physical manifestations.

3. **Holistic Therapies**: Integrative approaches such as Reiki, acupuncture, and chiropractic care can help in balancing the body's energy and relieving physical symptoms caused by emotional stress.

4. **Healthy Lifestyle Choices**: Adopting a balanced diet, regular exercise, and sufficient sleep can support both physical and emotional health, creating a strong foundation for overall well-being.

By embracing a holistic perspective that honors the mind-body connection, we can transform our approach to health and healing, fostering a life of harmony and vitality. Let us embark on this journey with compassion, awareness, and a deep reverence for the intricate interplay between our emotions and physical health.

The Lingering Impact of Grief on Physical Health

Grief is a profound emotional response to loss, whether it be the death of a loved one, **the end of a relationship**, or other significant life changes. When grief is held onto for an extended period without resolution, it can have a deep and detrimental impact on physical health. Here, we explore how prolonged grief can manifest in various health issues throughout the body.

1. Cardiovascular Health

Heart Disease and High Blood Pressure

- **Impact**: Prolonged grief can elevate stress levels, leading to increased blood pressure and heart rate.

Over time, this chronic stress can contribute to the development of hypertension and increase the risk of heart disease.

- **Symptoms**: Chest pain, palpitations, and shortness of breath are common physical manifestations.

Broken Heart Syndrome (Takotsubo Cardiomyopathy)

- **Impact**: Intense grief can lead to a temporary condition known as Broken Heart Syndrome, where the heart's left ventricle weakens and bulges, mimicking a heart attack.
- **Symptoms**: Severe chest pain and shortness of breath, often triggered by extreme emotional stress.

2. Immune System

Weakened Immune Response

- **Impact**: Chronic grief can suppress the immune system, making the body more susceptible to infections and illnesses.
- **Symptoms**: Frequent colds, flu, and slower recovery times from illnesses.

Inflammatory Disorders

- **Impact**: Persistent stress and grief can lead to chronic inflammation, which is linked to various autoimmune diseases.

- **Symptoms**: Joint pain, fatigue, and flare-ups of autoimmune conditions such as rheumatoid arthritis or lupus.

3. Digestive System

Gastrointestinal Disorders

- **Impact**: Grief affects the gut-brain axis, leading to digestive issues such as irritable bowel syndrome (IBS), gastritis, and acid reflux.
- **Symptoms**: Stomach pain, bloating, nausea, and changes in bowel habits.

Appetite Changes

- **Impact**: Grief can significantly alter eating habits, leading to weight loss or weight gain. Some may lose their appetite entirely, while others may turn to food for comfort.
- **Symptoms**: Rapid weight fluctuations, nutritional deficiencies, and related health problems.

4. Respiratory System

Respiratory Issues

- **Impact**: The emotional pain of grief can lead to physical tension in the chest and diaphragm, causing breathing difficulties.
- **Symptoms**: Shortness of breath, hyperventilation, and exacerbation of conditions like asthma.

5. Musculoskeletal System

Muscle Tension and Pain

- **Impact**: Chronic grief can cause persistent muscle tension, leading to pain and stiffness in various parts of the body, particularly the neck, shoulders, and back.
- **Symptoms**: Muscle aches, joint pain, and tension headaches.

Fibromyalgia

- **Impact**: Grief can trigger or exacerbate fibromyalgia, a condition characterized by widespread musculoskeletal pain.
- **Symptoms**: Chronic pain, fatigue, sleep disturbances, and cognitive difficulties.

6. Nervous System

Chronic Stress Response

- **Impact**: Prolonged grief keeps the body in a state of heightened stress, which affects the nervous system and can lead to anxiety disorders and depression.
- **Symptoms**: Constant fatigue, irritability, insomnia, and panic attacks.

Neurological Disorders

- **Impact**: Long-term stress and grief can increase the risk of developing neurological conditions such as migraines and tension headaches.
- **Symptoms**: Severe headache pain, light sensitivity, and nausea.

7. Endocrine System

Hormonal Imbalance

- **Impact**: Chronic grief can disrupt the production of hormones, leading to issues such as thyroid dysfunction and adrenal fatigue.
- **Symptoms**: Weight changes, fatigue, mood swings, and irregular menstrual cycles.

8. Skin and Hair

Skin Conditions

- **Impact**: Stress and grief can lead to skin issues such as acne, eczema, and psoriasis.
- **Symptoms**: Rashes, breakouts, and itchy, inflamed skin.

Hair Loss

- **Impact**: Prolonged emotional stress can disrupt the hair growth cycle, leading to conditions like telogen effluvium, where hair falls out more easily.

- **Symptoms**: Noticeable hair thinning or loss.

Addressing Grief for Better Health

Recognizing the profound impact of grief on physical health is the first step towards healing. Here are some ways to address and mitigate the effects of prolonged grief:

1. **Seek Professional Help**: Therapy, counselling, and support groups can provide a safe space to process grief.

2. **Practice Mindfulness and Meditation**: These techniques can help manage stress and promote emotional healing.

3. **Maintain a Healthy Lifestyle**: Balanced nutrition, regular exercise, and sufficient sleep are crucial for physical and emotional well-being.

4. **Express Emotions**: Journaling, art, and talking with trusted friends or family members can help release suppressed emotions.

5. **Engage in Relaxation Techniques**: Activities like yoga, deep breathing exercises, and Reiki can reduce physical tension and promote relaxation.

By addressing grief holistically and with compassion, we can foster healing that encompasses both the mind and body, leading to a healthier, more balanced life.

Mediations

Finding Peace Within: Meditation for Healing Emotional Trauma

Emotional trauma can leave deep scars, impacting our daily lives and relationships creating greater impact on our performance, while therapy can be a powerful tool, meditation offers a powerful, complementary approach to healing.

In the early chapters I have mentioned about Alpha and Theta state which are very helpful to focus, create opportunities and heal. I would recommend each individual to practice meditation for at least 20 minutes, if not 20 minutes for 10 minutes at least.

The Silent Toll: Mental and Emotional Health in the Workplace

The relentless pursuit of success in the workplace often comes at a cost – our mental and emotional well-being. We push through long hours, juggle demanding deadlines, and prioritize productivity over personal well-being. However, this neglect has a silent and insidious consequence: it can have a profound impact on our long-term health, including the development of Alzheimer's disease and other mental illnesses.

The Delayed Impact:

Research suggests that the effects of neglecting mental and emotional health during work can take decades to manifest. Studies have shown a link between chronic work stress and an increased risk of developing Alzheimer's disease later in life. Similarly, unaddressed anxiety and depression can exacerbate cognitive decline as we age.

Beyond Brain issues

The impact of neglecting mental and emotional health goes beyond Alzheimer's disease. Chronic stress can contribute to a variety of mental health issues, it is said is Stress might be one of the contributors to Alzheimer's, most importantly when we neglect our eating habits, on time and eating good diet food is very essential in order to have a great mental health.

Practising Breathing techniques, Yoga and meditation will help in reviving your mental and emotional health

Taking Action:

It's never too late to prioritize your mental and emotional health. Here are some steps you can take:

- **Stress Management Techniques:** Practice mindfulness meditation, deep breathing exercises, or yoga to reduce stress and promote relaxation.
- **Healthy Eating Habits:** Fuel your body with nutritious meals and snacks to maintain energy levels and cognitive function.
- **Work-Life Balance:** Set boundaries between work and personal life. Disconnect from work emails and calls after hours and make time for activities you enjoy.

- **Seek Support:** Don't be afraid to seek professional help for anxiety, depression, or other mental health concerns.

Benefits of Meditation for Emotional Trauma:

- **Reduced Stress and Anxiety:** Meditation helps regulate the nervous system, promoting relaxation and reducing symptoms of anxiety and stress commonly associated with emotional trauma.
- **Improved Emotional Regulation:** By increasing awareness of your thoughts and emotions, meditation allows you to observe them without judgment and respond rather than react.
- **Enhanced Self-Compassion:** Meditation cultivates a sense of kindness towards yourself, promoting self-acceptance and forgiveness, crucial for healing from trauma.
- **Increased Focus and Clarity:** Meditation trains your mind to focus on the present moment, reducing rumination on past experiences.

Healing Trauma Meditation:

This meditation is designed to create a safe space for you to connect with yourself and begin the healing process. Find a quiet, comfortable place where you won't be disturbed. Sit or lie down in a relaxed position, closing your eyes gently.

1. **Body Scan (5 minutes):**
   - Begin by taking a few slow, deep breaths, feeling your belly rise and fall with each inhalation and exhalation.
   - Bring your awareness to your body, starting with your toes. Notice any sensations without judgment - warmth, coolness, tension, or relaxation.
   - Slowly scan your body, moving your awareness upwards, noticing sensations in your legs, feet, hands, arms, torso, and head.
   - Acknowledge any areas of tension and consciously relax those muscles.

2. **Breath Awareness (5 minutes):**
   - Focus your attention on your breath. Feel the coolness of the air entering your nostrils and the warmth leaving as you exhale.
   - Don't force your breath, simply observe it naturally. If your mind wanders, gently bring your attention back to your breath.

3. **Visualization (5 minutes):**
   - Imagine yourself in a safe and peaceful place. It could be a real or imagined location, a place that brings you comfort and a sense of calm.
   - Visualize the details of this place - the sights, sounds, smells. Engage all your senses to create a vivid picture in your mind.

- Feel the sense of peace and security in this safe space.

4. **Compassion (5 minutes):**
   - Focus on yourself with kindness and understanding. Imagine a warm, gentle light surrounding you.
   - Silently repeat a mantra of self-compassion, such as "May I be filled with peace," or "May I be kind to myself."
   - Allow feelings of compassion and self-love to wash over you.

5. **Returning to the Present (5 minutes):**
   - Gently wiggle your fingers and toes, noticing the sensations in your body.
   - Take a few slow, deep breaths, bringing your awareness back to the present moment.
   - When you're ready, slowly open your eyes and take a moment to integrate the experience.

Remember:
- Be patient with yourself. It takes practice to develop a meditation practice.
- If difficult emotions arise, observe them without judgment and gently return your focus to your breath or your safe space.
- Meditation is a journey, not a destination. Enjoy the process of inner exploration and healing.

Additional Tips:

- Start with shorter meditation sessions (5-10 minutes) and gradually increase the duration as you become more comfortable.
- Consider incorporating guided meditations specifically designed for emotional healing.
- There are many resources available online and through apps to support your meditation practice.

By making meditation a regular practice, you can create a safe space for healing, fostering emotional resilience and inner peace on your journey to well-being.

This meditation is very powerful and helps you to calm down your stress, anxiety, fear or any other component.

Release & Renew: A 7-Minute Meditation for Letting Go

This meditation will guide you through a process of releasing negative emotions and limiting beliefs, creating space for positive change.

Preparation (1 minute):

- Find a quiet, comfortable place where you won't be disturbed.
- Sit or lie down in a relaxed position. Close your eyes and take a few deep breaths, inhaling slowly through your nose and exhaling completely through your mouth. Feel your body soften with each exhale.

Anchoring in the Present (1 minute):

- Bring your attention to the present moment. Notice the sounds around you, the feeling of your breath, and the sensations in your body. This is your anchor point throughout the meditation.

Identifying Negative Emotions (1 minute):

- Gently turn your attention inward. Acknowledge any negative emotions you might be holding onto - anger, frustration, sadness, fear, etc. Don't judge them, simply observe them with curiosity.

- Imagine these emotions as colored balls of light within your body. Notice where you feel them most intensely.

Visualization for Release (2 minutes):

- Visualize each ball of negative emotion expanding and becoming lighter. Imagine them floating upwards, out of your body, and towards a radiant source of white light above you.

- As they reach the light, see them dissolving and transforming into pure, white light. This light filters back down into you, nourishing your body and mind with positive energy.

Letting Go of Limiting Beliefs (1 minute):

- Now, focus on any limiting beliefs you might have - negative thoughts about yourself or your capabilities. These could be beliefs like "I'm not good enough," "I can't succeed," or "I don't deserve happiness."

- Visualize these beliefs written on pieces of paper. With each exhale, imagine the paper crumbling and dissolving, releasing the hold these beliefs have on you.

Affirmations for Renewal (1 minute):

- Replace the negative emotions and beliefs with positive affirmations. Silently repeat affirmations like:
    - "I am worthy of love and happiness."
    - "I am capable of achieving my goals."
    - "I release the past and embrace positive change."
    - Chant this number that will dissolve your fear and stress 1193 2291 333. This number needs to be spelled individually, do not say double one or double two, instead you need to spell this number as one one nine three two two nine one three three three, chant this number for 1 to 2 mins or as long as you can chant, you will experience the power of this quantum healing number

- Feel the positive energy of these affirmations fill your being.

Bringing it Back (1 minute):

- Slowly begin to bring your awareness back to your breath. Notice how you feel now compared to the beginning of the meditation.
- Take a few deep breaths and gently wiggle your fingers and toes. When you're ready, open your eyes, carrying the feeling of renewed energy and positive perspective with you.

Always end meditation by saying Thank you, thank you thank you three times, gently rub your palms and tough your palms to your eyes. Open your eyes as and when you feel like

The process of rubbing palms is required in order to awaken our muscles that have gone off to sleep and bring us back from meditations

Whenever you get into deep state of meditation you might experience immense energy levels and will not feel like opening your eyes, allow the energy to subside and again rub your palms and tough your palms to your eye

You can also say "I am Centered in Safety all my energies and bodies are integrated into me now", repeat this sentence three times you will feel grounded

Slip into Theta state – Healing State

This technique helps you to slip into a deeper state of meditation and helps you to heal your physical, emotional, mental bodies

Choose any of the above meditation techniques and once you have completed the meditation you and before you rub your palms and touch your palms to your eyes you need to do the below steps, Breathe Deeply for

1. 13 breaths
2. 8 breaths
3. 5 breaths
4. 3 breaths
5. 2 breaths
6. once

This will help you to slip into theta state. You can get numb and your breathing too would slow down helping you to relax completely and feel rejuvenated

Once you are out of the meditation you need to rub your palms and touch your palms to your eyes.

Say the below statement thrice

I am fully and completely centred in myself, all my energies and bodies are integrated into me now, I am in my energy field now, Thank you thank you thank you

Power Words for Daily Transformation

We offer you Powerful words for daily transformation, these are called Switch words. These Switch words help in harnessing the Subconscious Mind

The Role of Conscious, Subconscious, and Superconscious Minds

Our conscious mind can manifest up to 10% of our desires, while the subconscious mind has the potential to manifest up to 70%. The superconscious mind can influence the remaining 20%. This indicates that affirmations, which primarily engage the conscious mind, take longer to manifest. To activate the subconscious mind and expedite the manifestation process, we use **Switch words**.

Understanding Switch words

Switch words are powerful words that connect directly with the subconscious mind, directing it to draw the essence of the word to you. Repeating a Switch word increases its positive impact on your energy, thereby attracting the experiences, conditions, or responses the word represents.

How Switch words Work

Switch words act as triggers, activating the subconscious mind and helping override blockages. They create shortcuts to deliver what we desire by bypassing conscious resistance.

Using Switchwords Effectively

To achieve the most effective outcome with Switchwords, it's crucial to maintain a high vibrational state. Here's how to use them:

1. **Elevate Your Emotional State**: Engage in activities that uplift your vibrations, such as deep breathing, guided meditations, dancing, or listening to upbeat music.

2. **Set Your Intention**: Clearly define what you want to manifest, such as healing, financial abundance, academic success, improved relationships, etc.

3. **Maintain a Positive Emotional State**: Spend 20 to 30 minutes in a positive state to speed up manifestation.

4. **Write Switch words on Your Body**: Use your non-dominant hand or the opposite side if you are left-handed.

5. **Place Switch words on Paper**: Paste them on your body or place them under your bed to work while you sleep.

6. **Create Healing Circles**: Amplify the power of Switch words by creating energy circles.

7. **Use Switch words in Various Forms**: Write them on doors, water bottles, coasters, or medicine boxes.

Benefits of Switch words

Switch words can help:

- Alleviate pain, low mood, and stress
- Break negative habits
- Promote sleep and peace of mind
- Inspire creativity and problem-solving
- Boost leadership qualities
- Manifest money
- Attract love and friendship
- Deepen relationship bonds
- Assist in education and study
- Support healing

Methods to Use Switch words

Switch words can be intended through:

- Thought
- Chanting
- Speech
- Singing
- Mantras

You can chant Switch words 10, 28, or 108 times or for as long as they make you feel good.

Calibrating Your Mind

Before starting with Switch words, calibrate your conscious and subconscious mind by using the master Switch word, **"TOGETHER"**.

1. **Chant "TOGETHER"**: Relax your body, take deep breaths, and chant "TOGETHER" 28 or 108 times, or for 5-7 minutes.

2. **Repeat for Three Days**: Do this for three consecutive days to integrate your conscious and subconscious minds, enhancing the effectiveness of subsequent Switchwords.

Example of Using Switch words

Suppose you want to heal your body. After calibrating your mind with "TOGETHER" for three days, you can start using a specific Switch word like "BE-DIVINE-HEALTH."

1. Elevate your emotional state.

2. Set your intention to heal your body.

3. Chant "TOGETHER BE-DIVINE-HEALTH" while in a positive state.

4. Repeat as often as needed, maintaining a high vibrational state.

By following these steps, you can harness the power of your subconscious mind to manifest your desires more effectively and efficiently.

Now from first day you can also chant the below switch words

1. Together Divine Light Envelope - this means to protect and shield you
2. Together Divine Light Heal - this means to Heal you
3. Together Find Divine Count on Now – to get money with miracles, Find
4. Together Bow Love Restore – Bow makes the feeling smaller; Love generates Self Love and Restore brings confidence
5. Release Resistance, Together Change Together – Release Resistance clears the self-confidence issues and Together Change clears away whatever you don't want or need.

Practical Examples for Working Professionals

Morning Routine: Start your day with words like Together FOCUS (repeat for 10 times) and Together ENERGY UP, UP UP, UP (repeat for 10 times) to set a positive tone for the day.

Before Meetings: Use Together Focus (repeat 10 times), Together CONFIDENCE or Together SUCCESS (repeat 10 times) to prepare for critical presentations.

During Work Stress: Repeat Together CALM (repeat 10 times) or Together PEACE (repeat 10 times) to ground yourself during high-pressure tasks.

Similarly, we have provided a list of impactful switchwords when repeatedly chanted gives amazing results

ACT: If you would like to become a good speaker.

ADD: This is to increase what you have, no matter what it is.

ADJUST: This is a great one to create balance in your life. It will also help you handle uncomfortable or unpleasant conditions.

ALONE: This will help you nurture or heal yourself or another. This will help you increase focus on yourself but not in a self absorbed way but in terms of nurturing and healing yourself.

AROUND: This will help you gain or improve your perspective.

ATTENTION: This will help you do detailed work and avoid carelessness. This will apply to other areas of your life as well, not only work.

BE: This is a powerful one, this will help you to achieve peace and good health. it will help you have good form; dispel loneliness; increase your skill in sports. it also has the added benefit of helping you brush off ridicule from others.

BETWEEN: This one is often used to develop intuition and psychic abilities. It works.

BLUFF: This one is good to get rid of nervousness or fear as well as increase your imagination. It is especially good to use when you want to create pleasant dreams.

BOW: This helps reduce any arrogant tendencies you may have.

BRING: This is a manifestation Switchword, it helps you unite with your goal, helps you finish what you started.

BUBBLE: This Switchword is really good at helping you expand your perceived limits, it is also good for creating a mood of excitement and energy.

CANCEL: Use this Switchword to eliminate negative thoughts and conditions. It helps eliminate debt, poverty and other unwanted conditions. Which in turn will dispel worry. I use this one when I feel insecure about something.

CANCER: To clarify, this does not mean cancer the disease but rather the zodiac sign. This Switchword is used to calm emotional distress and to soften outlook.

CARE: This one is used to help you retain or memorize anything you need to remember or retain. You can say it before you read something so as to remember it.

CHANGE: This helps get rid of emotional and physical pain. It also helps get something out of the eye.

CHARLTON HESTON: I admit, I feel silly saying this one sometimes but it is good to keep you mindful about your posture. Helps you stand straight and tall. You can use someone else names who stands straight or tall with confidence.

CHARM: This will help you manifest your heart's desire.

CHLORINE: This will help you mingle and share yourself with others. Helps you make a difference; blend in and become one with.

CHUCKLE: This one helps you turn on personality.

CIRCULATE: This helps you end loneliness and helps you feel at ease so you can mingle with people.

CLASSIC: Use this one to appear cultured and suave.

CLEAR: This one will help you dispel anger and resentment you may towards yourself or others.

CLIMB: This will help you enhance your view point, rise above it all.

CONCEDE: This helps to reconcile and end arguments between people. You can use it if you want to be at peace with someone.

CONFESS: This ends aggression very well.

CONTINUE: This helps create or increase endurance for both physical and mental tasks.

COPY: this helps you have good taste and also increases fertility.

COUNT: This will help you make money and help you reduce or stop smoking

COVER: reduce nervousness; subdue inner excitement

CRISP: This is a great one to dispel fatigue, feel refreshed, revitalizes. It also helps brighten your mood.

CROWD: This helps reduce or eliminate disobedience in children, pets or subordinate's ant work.

CRYSTAL: This is a powerful Switch word that will help you clarify any situation or things. It helps you look to the future; both mentally and through clairvoyance. This can help you access Universal Knowledge. I use this one to clarify intentions when I feel blocked.

CURVE: This helps to create beauty; make something beautiful. This is good to enhance creativity.

CUT: This will help you achieve moderation in all your actions. it can also help you make proactive decisions regarding toxic relationships. Essentially giving you the strength to sever ties with a toxic person if you have to.

CUTE: This will help you think; discern; be sharp-witted and be clever.

DEDICATE: This will help you to stop clinging to either a person or a situation.

DIVINE: This one will help you work miracles or accomplish extraordinary things, it increases personal ability.

DIVINE LIGHT: This will help you focus on positivity, multiply the intensity of any thought; increase spiritual enlightenment.

DIVINE ORDER: This will help you with any organizing or cleaning you need to do. It helps you be more efficient making sure things are in optimal order. I use this when I feel disorganized with my thoughts or do not know where to start something. It helps bring order.
DO: eliminate procrastination in its tracks with this one.

DONE: This is a great one against procrastination as well, it helps you meet a deadline or keep a resolution. It's great for building will power.

DOWN: This helps you become more humble. People don't like braggarts, this will help eliminate that trait in you if bragging is a problem for you.

DUCK: This helps dispel sensitivity about looks or capabilities. Helps you shrug off criticism.

ELATE: This helps transform a setback into a positive uplifting event.

FIGHT: This helps you win a competitive game and intensify your efforts and intentions.

FIND: This helps you build a fortune and can be used with Switch word "COUNT".

FOR: This will help you promote anything.

FOREVER: This will help you keep a secret.

FORGIVE: This will help you cool your anger and end desire for revenge. This also helps dispel remorse.

FULL: This helps you achieve optimum levels to help you go beyond and expand your capacity in any endeavor.

GIGGLE: This will get you in the mood for writing. It will also help you enjoy the task at hand.

GIVE: To sell something and to help others.

GO: This will help you end laziness. Helps you begin and progress in anything. I use it when I feel like I don't want to start something right away. I say GO and I get motivated.

GUARD: This helps protect you from bodily hard, spirit or your property. it helps to preserve your personal safety.

HALFWAY: This helps make a long distance seem short. This is one of 3 Switch words I use to make my long runs easier. it also helps me better handle projects that require long tedious work.

HELP: This helps eliminate indecision or uncertainty and increases focus.

HO: Saying this one helps you relax and reduce tension.

HOLD: This helps to build character.

HOLE: This will help create attractiveness and sex appeal in yourself.

HORSE: This will help you be solid, strong and gain personal power.

HORSE SHOE: This will help you remain steadfast and strengthen the soul during times of challenge. It will help you safely move rapidly ahead and remain sturdy throughout.

JUDGE: This will help you love reading and increase your comprehension of what you read. I use this all the time when I read.

LEARN: act and be youthful; rejuvenate your mind and soul.

LIGHT: This will help you be inspired, lighten the load or mood. It's a great stress reducer.

LIMIT: set parameters, regain control. This will help keep others from taking advantage of you.

LISTEN: This will help you predict the future. This is also very powerful when you want to get in touch with nature and yourself.

LOVE: This will help generate, radiate and experience love of all types.

MAGNANIMITY: This will help you eliminate pettiness and increase generosity. MASK: Protect and shield from harm.

MONA LISA: This will help bring a smile to your face and dispel hatred and envy. (Or you can use someone who represents a smile to you)

MOVE: This is great to increase energy and eliminate tiredness. It is one of the 3 words I use every time I run, without fail.

NEXT: This will help you finish lots of meticulous work and be able to endure more.

NOW: This ends procrastination. It also helps you to act on good impulses.

OFF: This one is used to quit an unwanted habit AND it helps you go to sleep. This Switchword does help me sleep. If I wake up in the middle of the night, I can rely on "OFF" to help me get back to sleep quickly. I love it.

OFFER: This will help dispel greed.

OIL: This will help external and internal friction. Smooth and release tensions and resistance.

ON: This is a very powerful Switchword to help you get new ideas; obtain transportation; nourish your ambition.

OPEN: This will he help you inhibitions. It will increase tolerance and understanding. It can free the mind and allow feeling and ideas to flow easily. OVER: This will help end frustration.

PERSONAL: This will help you be a success. it will help you publish a successful newspaper or a newsletter or book for that matter.

PHASE: This will help you set goals. Set a routine or pattern and improve your situation.

POINT: This will improve eyesight and focus. it will help you find direction and make a clear decision.

POSTPONE: This helps you to let things go.

PRAISE: This will help you be beautiful or handsome and will help you to stop being overly critical with yourself.

PUT: This will help you build and expand. You can use this for any endeavour you want to build or expand.

QUIET: This will help quiet the ego. If you feel you must get the last word in, say QUIET and you will notice how that urge will subside. I used this the other day and I was able to just let it all go and let the other person have their moment.

REACH: This is great to locate misplaced objects and reach solutions for problems. It will help you repair things. It will help you recall forgotten ideas and information in your mind or memory like names, numbers etc. I used this twice and it worked very well. I am not one to lose my keys, in fact, I NEVER DO. When I did, I used this Switch word and I found it very quickly and in the most unlikely place. The fridge. (I have no idea how they got in there).

REJOICE: When you encounter someone who is more successful in something that you want success in, it is easy to feel jealous. This Switch word will help dispel jealousy.

RESCIND: This will help you undo; restart; cancel; redo; something. Some other teachers of Switch words recommend that this switch word should Always be used with the Switch words; BETWEEN, CRYSTAL and LISTEN in order to avoid as they say "possible time loop." I can't say I know exactly what that means, but erring on the side of caution can't hurt.

RESTORE: This will help restore fairness and honesty.

REVERSE: This will help you get rid of grudges or stop a repetitive pattern in the moment.

RIDICULOUS: This will help you gain a lot of attention.

ROOT: This will help you discover and grow in any area of your life.

SAGE: To help you dispel evil in the mind or your home.

SAVE: This will help you stop drinking alcohol and other unwanted habits. I used this word with POSTPONE to help me when I was drinking a lot.

SCHEME: This is great for those of you who want to advertise, design and create marketing plans or PR for your company or business. SHOW: This will help you raise your moral standards and help you develop respect for people and yourself.

SHUT: When you feel a bit reckless and sad, use this to help you stop looking for trouble.

SHUTUP AND FORGET – if you tend to go on any old memory lane

SOPHISTICATE: This will help you publish a successful magazine or book. It will also help you become a great success

SPEND: This will help you develop a sense of style.

STRETCH: This will help you prolong a good feeling, event or a sense of well-being you are experiencing. It will also help you grow intellectually, spiritually and physically. By grow I mean become better.

SWEET: This will help you be soothing and caring to others.

SWING: This will raise your courage and boldness.

SWIVEL: relieve constipation and diarrhea. All I am going to say about this one is that...it works.

TAKE: This will help you become a good leader. This is great for people who find that they need to develop leadership skills quickly.

TAP: This will help you convert; adapt; renovate anything.

THANKS: This will help increase gratitude in your heart and will help release guilt.

TINY: This will help you be polite, kind hearted and courteous. It will also you decrease the importance of something that bothers you.

TOMORROW: This will help you eliminate remorse and sorrow.

UNMASK: This Switch word will help bring things into focus; expose; lay bare before you.

UP: This will help elevate your mood and help you defeat feelings of inferiority.

WAIT: Saying this will create a situation where you will learn a secret.

WASTE: This will help you appear rich and show opulence.

WATCH: This will help you learn a skill or perfect a skill you already have.

WITH: This will help you be agreeable and compatible with others.

WOMB: This will help you attract and feel cuddled and safe. This will help you reconnect with Divinity and Mother Nature.

ON - for creating new ideas

LEARN - to stay looking and feeling young

FIGHT - to win a game or contest

MOVE - for an increase in energy and vitality

CARE - to remember needed information

WATCH - to gain a wanted skill or ability

TINY - to be a kinder person

THANKS - to stop regretting the past

ADJUST - to handle an unwanted experience

NOW - to take action on an impulse

DONE - to develop willpower

DO - to stop procrastinating

FOR - for promoting something

SCHEME - to advertise something

STRETCH - to feel good and have well being

GUARD - to promote personal safety

PRAISE - to make yourself attractive

OFF - to fall asleep

TAKE - to become a leader

SWING - to develop courage

BE - To maintain good health; To banish lonesomeness; To achieve peace of conscience

The Switch words above are all effective. You can mix and match them as you please.

Some more examples of how we can club Switch Words

TOGETHER REACH RIDICULOUS – to promote creatively as a team

TOGETHER SCHEME RIDICULOUS – To produce and sell, also called as Entrepreneurs switch word

RELEASE RESISTANCE TOGETHER CHANGE NOW

TOGETHER DIVINE LIGHT ADJUST – to harmonize chakras

TOGETHER DIVINE ORDER – for chakra alignment

TOGETHER SHAKTI DIVINE FLOWER – to open chakra

TOGETHER SHAKTI FOREVER – to close chakra

TOGETHER SHAKTI PURE CRYSTAL HALFWAY – To keep the crown and third eye chakra partially open.

TOGETHER DIVINE HUM – This will synchronize vibration of chakras.

Chakras

Let us explore the fascinating world of chakras, the energy centre's that play a crucial role in our physical, emotional, and spiritual well-being. Whether you're new to the concept or looking to deepen your understanding, this session will guide you through the basics and significance of each chakra.

Our body has total 543 chakras, out of which seven chakras are placed in our center pillar of our body which are actually drivers of the specific organ system.

What Are Chakras?

The Chakras are spinning wheels of energy located along the spine, from the base to the crown of the head. There are seven main chakras, each associated with different aspects of our being. When these chakras are balanced and aligned, energy flows freely, promoting health and harmony. Conversely, blocked or imbalanced chakras can lead to physical and emotional issues.

Blocked energy in our seven chakras can often lead to illness, loss of opportunities, loss of energy levels over all our vibrations go low, so it's important to understand what each chakra represents Refer the picture below, this picture depicts the seven chakras in our body, each indicating its importance.

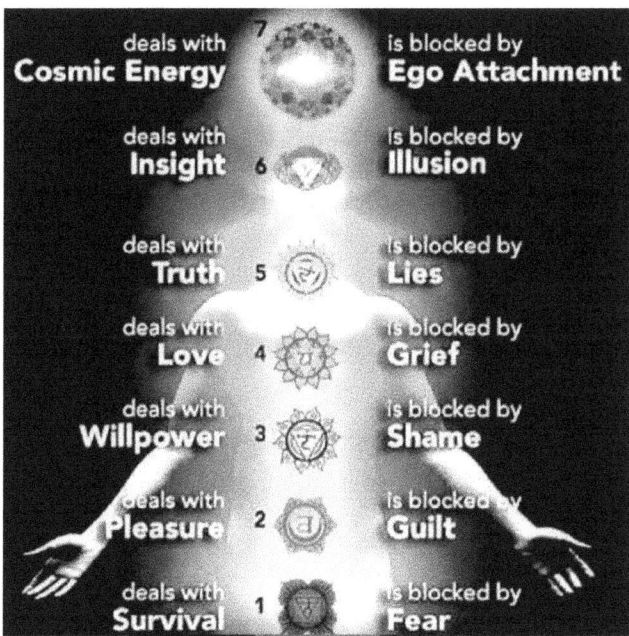

Frequency Chart for Organs

Organ/System	Frequency (Hz)
Brain	10 Hz (Alpha waves)
Heart	1-2 Hz
Lungs	72-78 Hz

Organ/System	Frequency (Hz)
Liver	60 Hz
Kidneys	10 Hz
Stomach	3-9 Hz
Intestines	3-5 Hz
Bladder	10 Hz
Blood Circulation	100-160 Hz
Bones	38-43 Hz
Skin	275 Hz
Thyroid	25 Hz
Pancreas	117 Hz
Spleen	10 Hz
Gall Bladder	164.3 Hz
Adrenal Glands	492.8 Hz

These frequencies are used in various holistic healing practices, including sound therapy, bio-resonance therapy, and vibrational medicine, to promote health and well-being by restoring balance and harmony within the body's energy systems.

What happens when the frequency of the organs are disturbed?

When the natural frequencies of organs are disturbed, it can lead to various physical, emotional, and psychological imbalances. Here are some potential effects:

General Effects of Disturbed Organ Frequencies

1. **Physical Health Issues:**
- **Pain and Discomfort:** Disruption in the frequency of an organ can lead to pain or discomfort in that area. For example, disturbances in the liver's frequency might cause liver pain or dysfunction.
- **Chronic Conditions:** Prolonged frequency disturbances can contribute to the development of chronic conditions, such as gastrointestinal disorders if the stomach and intestines' frequencies are affected.
- **Weakened Immune System:** Imbalances in the frequencies of organs involved in immune function, like the spleen and lymphatic system, can weaken the body's ability to fight infections and diseases.

2. **Emotional and Mental Health Issues:**
- **Stress and Anxiety:** Disruptions in the heart and brain frequencies can lead to increased stress and

anxiety levels. For example, an imbalance in the heart's frequency might manifest as emotional stress, while brainwave disturbances can lead to anxiety and restlessness.

- **Depression:** Long-term disturbances in the brain's frequencies, particularly those associated with mood regulation, can contribute to depression.

- **Cognitive Impairment:** Imbalances in brain frequencies can also affect cognitive functions, leading to issues with memory, focus, and overall mental clarity.

3. **Energy Blockages:**

- **Chakra Imbalances:** Each chakra is associated with specific organs and their frequencies. Disruptions can cause energy blockages, leading to physical and emotional symptoms. For example, an imbalance in the throat chakra can affect the thyroid and communication abilities.

- **Reduced Vitality:** When organ frequencies are disturbed, the flow of life force energy (often referred to as Qi or Prana) can be impeded, leading to a general sense of fatigue and lack of vitality.

Specific Organ Frequency Disturbances

1. **Brain:**

- **Insomnia:** Disrupted brain frequencies can interfere with sleep patterns, leading to insomnia or poor-quality sleep.

- **Headaches:** Frequency imbalances can cause headaches or migraines.

2. **Heart:**
- **Heart Disease:** Chronic disturbances in heart frequency can contribute to cardiovascular diseases, including arrhythmias and hypertension.
- **Emotional Imbalance:** Since the heart is closely linked to emotions, disturbances can lead to emotional instability.

3. **Lungs:**
- **Respiratory Issues:** Disturbed lung frequencies can lead to respiratory problems, such as asthma, bronchitis, or chronic obstructive pulmonary disease (COPD).

4. **Liver:**
- **Detoxification Problems:** The liver's primary function is detoxification. Frequency disturbances can impair this function, leading to toxin buildup in the body.
- **Digestive Issues:** As the liver is also involved in digestion, disturbances can cause digestive problems like bloating, constipation, or diarrhea.

5. **Kidneys:**
- **Fluid Imbalance:** The kidneys regulate fluid balance in the body. Frequency disturbances can lead to issues like edema or dehydration.
- **Kidney Stones:** Imbalances can increase the risk of developing kidney stones or other renal issues.

6. **Stomach and Intestines:**
- **Digestive Disorders:** Disturbed frequencies can lead to conditions like irritable bowel syndrome (IBS), acid reflux, or gastritis.
- **Nutrient Absorption Issues:** Frequency imbalances can affect the intestines' ability to absorb nutrients effectively, leading to deficiencies.

Restoring Frequency Balance

Restoring the natural frequencies of organs can help mitigate these issues and promote overall health and well-being. Some methods include:

- **Sound Therapy:** Using specific frequencies and sound waves to restore balance.
- **Energy Healing:** Practices like Reiki, acupuncture, and bio-resonance therapy.
- **Meditation and Mindfulness:** Techniques to calm the mind and restore brainwave balance.
- **Healthy Lifestyle Choices:** Proper nutrition, exercise, and stress management to support overall organ health.

In order to enhance your frequency, it is essential to meditate, below are the chakra mantra, by chanting these mantras for 7 times each you will experience the shift in your energy levels. Doing it consistently will help you to larger extent

1. Root Chakra — Represents our foundation and feeling of being grounded. Mantra is "LAM" or say it as "LAANG"

- **Location:** Base of spine in tailbone area.
- **Emotional issues:** Survival issues such as financial independence, money and food.
- **Health** – will heal health related issues such as lower spine, thighs, knees, calf or feet pain, balances over all energy which helps in centring ourselves

2. Sacral Chakra — Our connection and ability to accept others and new experiences. The mantra is "VAM" you can also say it as "VAAM"

- **Location:** Lower abdomen, about two inches below the navel and two inches in.
- **Emotional issues:** Sense of abundance, well-being, pleasure and sexuality.
- **Health** – Uterus, internal sex organs, ovaries, sperms, kidney lower spine related issues, helps in manifesting self worth

3. Solar Plexus Chakra — Our ability to be confident and in control of our lives. Matra is "RAM" or you can say it as "RAANG"

- **Location:** Upper abdomen in the stomach area.
- **Emotional issues:** Self-worth, self-confidence and self-esteem.

- **Health** – complete digestive system, wards off anxiety, fear, anger issues, grief

4. **Heart Chakra** — Our ability to love. Mantra is "YAM" or you can also say it as "YAANG"
   - **Location:** Center of chest just above the heart.
   - **Emotional issues:** Love, joy and inner peace.
   - **Health** – Lungs, Heart, shoulders, Thyroid glands, Thymus Glands, spondylitis can be cured

5. **Throat Chakra** — our ability to communicate. Mantra is "Hum" or say it as "HAANG"
   - **Location:** Throat.
   - **Emotional issues:** Communication, self-expression of feelings and the truth.
   - **Health** - Ear nose and throat related, breathing issues

6. **Third Eye Chakra** — Our ability to focus on and see the big picture. Mantra "OM" this is also called the BEEJ which needs to be said three times at a time, later increase it to five or seven times as convenient to you
   - **Location:** Forehead between the eyes (also called the Brow Chakra).
   - **Emotional issues:** Intuition, imagination, wisdom and the ability to think and make decisions.
   - **Health** - Eyes, Ear, Entire body balance, left brain

7. **Crown Chakra** — The highest chakra represents our ability to be fully connected spiritually. Mantra "AUM" also called as the Tree, it need to be chanted with "AaaaaaaaaaaaaOoooooooooommmm", when your breath holds the "O" on completion of breath you lips close ending it with "Mmmm"

- **Location:** The very top of the head.
- **Emotional issues:** Inner and outer beauty, our connection to spirituality and pure bliss.
- **Health – Entire body functioning, right brai**

Negativity removal techniques

Negativity can significantly impact your mental health, productivity, and overall well-being. Here are several techniques to help remove negativity from your life:

1. Practice Mindfulness and Meditation

Mindfulness Exercises: Focus on the present moment to reduce stress and anxiety.

- **Breathing Exercises**: Simple breathing techniques can calm your mind and reduce negative thoughts.
- **Body Scan Meditation**: Pay attention to different parts of your body to ground yourself and release tension.

Meditation Practices: Regular meditation can help you develop a more positive outlook.

- **Guided Meditations**: Use apps or online resources for guided sessions that focus on releasing negativity.
- **Loving-Kindness Meditation (Metta)**: Focus on sending love and kindness to yourself and others to cultivate a positive mindset.

2. Reframe Negative Thoughts

Cognitive Restructuring: Identify and challenge negative thought patterns.

- **Identify Negative Thoughts**: Write down your negative thoughts to understand their frequency and content.
- **Question Their Validity**: Ask yourself if these thoughts are based on facts or assumptions.
- **Replace with Positive Affirmations**: Develop positive statements to counter negative thoughts.

3. Surround Yourself with Positivity

Positive Relationships: Spend time with supportive, uplifting people.

- **Build a Support Network**: Cultivate relationships with friends, family, and colleagues who encourage and support you.
- **Limit Toxic Interactions**: Minimize time spent with people who drain your energy or bring negativity into your life.

Positive Environment: Create a space that fosters positivity.

- **Declutter Your Space**: A clean and organized environment can boost your mood.
- **Incorporate Positive Reminders**: Use inspirational quotes, pictures, and items that bring you joy.

4. Engage in Activities that Bring Joy

Hobbies and Interests: Spend time doing things you love.

- **Creative Activities**: Engage in activities like painting, writing, or playing music.
- **Physical Activities**: Exercise, dance, or practice yoga to release endorphins and improve your mood.

Volunteer and Help Others: Giving back can provide a sense of purpose and increase your positivity.

- **Community Service**: Volunteer for causes you care about.
- **Acts of Kindness**: Perform small acts of kindness in your daily life.

5. Practice Gratitude

Gratitude Journaling: Write down things you're thankful for each day.

- **Daily Entries**: Make it a habit to jot down at least three things you're grateful for every day.
- **Reflect on Positive Experiences**: Revisit your gratitude journal during challenging times to remind yourself of the good in your life.

Gratitude Exercises: Incorporate gratitude into your daily routine.

- **Gratitude Meditation**: Focus on things you're thankful for during your meditation practice.
- **Express Gratitude to Others**: Take time to thank people in your life who have positively impacted you.

6. Limit Negative Media Consumption

Reduce Exposure to Negative News: Limit the time spent consuming negative news or media.

SALT THE ULITMATE NEGATIVITY RELEASING AGENT

Yes, many people believe that salt can help in releasing negativity from the aura and providing relief. This practice has roots in various cultural and spiritual traditions, where salt is considered a purifying agent. Here are some common methods to use salt for this purpose:

1. Salt Baths

How It Helps: Salt baths are believed to cleanse the aura, remove negative energy, and promote relaxation.

How to Do It:

- **Ingredients**: Use sea salt, Epsom salt, or Himalayan pink salt.
- **Preparation**: Add 1-2 cups of salt to a warm bath.

- **Optional Additions**: You can also add essential oils like lavender or eucalyptus for added relaxation and healing.
- **Duration**: Soak in the bath for at least 20 minutes.
- **Visualization**: While soaking, visualize the salt drawing out negative energy from your body and aura.

2. Salt Scrubs

How It Helps: Using a salt scrub can exfoliate the skin and help remove negative energy.

How to Do It:

- **Ingredients**: Mix sea salt with a carrier oil like coconut or olive oil.
- **Application**: Gently scrub your body with the mixture in a circular motion.
- **Focus Areas**: Pay special attention to areas where you feel tension or negativity.
- **Rinse**: Rinse off with warm water, feeling the negativity wash away.

3. Salt Bowls

How It Helps: Placing bowls of salt around your living space can absorb negative energy.

How to Do It:

- **Ingredients**: Use small bowls filled with sea salt or Himalayan pink salt.

- **Placement**: Place the bowls in corners of rooms, near windows, or in areas where you feel negative energy accumulates.
- **Duration**: Leave the bowls for a few days to a week, then dispose of the salt.
- **Replacement**: Replace the salt regularly to maintain its effectiveness.

4. Salt Sprays

How It Helps: Salt sprays can be used to cleanse and refresh your space.

How to Do It:

- **Ingredients**: Dissolve a few tablespoons of sea salt in water and pour into a spray bottle.
- **Application**: Spray the solution around your home, particularly in areas where negative energy is felt.
- **Optional Additions**: Add a few drops of essential oils like sage or lavender for extra cleansing properties.

5. Salt Rituals

How It Helps: Performing a salt ritual can help you mentally and spiritually cleanse negativity.

How to Do It:

- **Ingredients**: Use sea salt or Himalayan pink salt.
- **Ritual Steps**:
  ➢ Stand in a quiet space and hold a handful of salt.

- ➤ Close your eyes and take a few deep breaths.
- ➤ Visualize the salt absorbing all negativity from your body and aura.
- ➤ As you feel the negativity being drawn out, slowly let the salt fall from your hands.
- ➤ Dispose of the salt away from your living space.

6. Salt Lamps

How It Helps: Himalayan salt lamps are believed to purify the air and improve energy. Keep one on your desk or nearby to cleanse the energies

How to Do It:

- **Placement**: Place salt lamps in areas where you spend a lot of time, such as the living room or bedroom.
- **Usage**: Keep the lamp on regularly to continuously benefit from its purifying properties.

The Productivity Boost in Every Drop

Aroma oils (essential oils) can help in removing negativity and overcoming stress. Aromatherapy, the use of essential oils for therapeutic purposes, has been practiced for centuries and is known for its ability to promote relaxation, reduce anxiety, and improve overall well-being. Here are a few essential oils that are particularly effective:

Essential Oils for Removing Negativity and Overcoming Stress

1. **Lavender**

    - **Benefits**: Lavender is well-known for its calming and relaxing properties. It helps reduce stress, anxiety, and promotes restful sleep.
    - **Usage**: Diffuse in a room, add a few drops to a bath, or apply diluted oil to your pulse points.

2. **Frankincense**

    - **Benefits**: Frankincense has grounding and purifying properties. It helps reduce stress and anxiety and promotes a sense of inner peace.

- **Usage**: Diffuse in a room, inhale directly from the bottle, or add to a carrier oil for massage.

3. **Rosemary**
   - **Benefits**: Rosemary is known for its ability to clear the mind and enhance mental clarity. It helps reduce stress and improve concentration.
   - **Usage**: Diffuse in a room, add to a bath, or inhale directly from the bottle.

4. **Peppermint**
   - **Benefits**: Peppermint has invigorating and uplifting properties. It helps alleviate stress and mental fatigue, promoting a sense of clarity and focus.
   - **Usage**: Diffuse in a room, inhale directly from the bottle, or apply diluted oil to your temples and neck.

5. **Bergamot**
   - **Benefits**: Bergamot has mood-lifting and calming properties. It helps reduce anxiety, stress, and feelings of depression.
   - **Usage**: Diffuse in a room, add to a bath, or apply diluted oil to your pulse points.

6. **Lemon**
   - **Benefits**: Lemon essential oil is refreshing and uplifting. It helps reduce feelings of negativity and promotes a positive mood.

- **Usage**: Diffuse in a room, inhale directly from the bottle, or add a few drops to a spray bottle with water to freshen up your space.

7. **Eucalyptus**
    - **Benefits**: Eucalyptus has purifying and clarifying properties. It helps clear negative energy and promotes mental clarity.
    - **Usage**: Diffuse in a room, add to a bath, or inhale directly from the bottle.

8. **Ylang Ylang**
    - **Benefits**: Ylang ylang has calming and balancing properties. It helps reduce stress and anxiety and promotes a sense of well-being.
    - **Usage**: Diffuse in a room, add to a bath, or apply diluted oil to your pulse points.

9. **Sandalwood**
    - **Benefits**: Sandalwood has grounding and calming properties. It helps reduce anxiety and stress and promotes a sense of inner peace.
    - **Usage**: Diffuse in a room, inhale directly from the bottle, or add to a carrier oil for massage.

10. **Patchouli**
    - **Benefits**: Patchouli has grounding and balancing properties. It helps reduce stress and anxiety and promotes a sense of well-being.

- **Usage**: Diffuse in a room, add to a bath, or apply diluted oil to your pulse points.

How to Use Essential Oils

1. **Diffusion**: Use an essential oil diffuser to disperse the aroma throughout your room. This method is excellent for creating a calming environment.

2. **Inhalation**: Inhale the aroma directly from the bottle or place a few drops on a tissue or cotton ball and inhale.

3. **Topical Application**: Dilute essential oils with a carrier oil (such as coconut, jojoba, or almond oil) and apply to your pulse points, such as wrists, temples, and neck.

4. **Bath**: Add a few drops of essential oil to your bathwater to create a relaxing and stress-relieving soak.

5. **Massage**: Mix essential oils with a carrier oil and use for a soothing massage to relieve tension and promote relaxation

Help Others

How Can Working Professionals Help Themselves by Helping Others?

Helping others can be a powerful way for working professionals to improve their own well-being and career success. This practice, often referred to as altruism, can have profound positive effects on mental health, job satisfaction, and personal growth. Here are several ways in which helping others can benefit working professionals:

1. Enhanced Emotional Well-being

When professionals assist others, whether colleagues, clients, or members of their community, they often experience a sense of fulfilment and happiness. This emotional uplift comes from the intrinsic reward of knowing they've made a positive impact. Research has shown that acts of kindness release endorphins, the brain's natural painkillers, and increase levels of oxytocin, the "love hormone," which enhances feelings of connection and reduces stress.

2. Improved Mental Health

Helping others can act as a buffer against mental health issues like depression and anxiety. Engaging in altruistic activities can shift focus away from personal stressors and provide a sense of purpose. This redirection can help alleviate feelings of isolation and sadness. Additionally, it promotes social interactions, which are vital for mental health, providing support networks and a sense of belonging.

3. Strengthened Professional Networks

Professionals who help others often find their efforts reciprocated, leading to stronger professional networks. By offering support and assistance to colleagues, they can foster a collaborative and supportive work environment. This reciprocity can lead to new opportunities, mentorship, and professional growth. Networking through helping can also build a reputation for being reliable and resourceful, which can open doors to career advancement.

4. Skill Development

Helping others often requires the use of various skills such as problem-solving, communication, and empathy. By regularly engaging in altruistic activities, professionals can hone these skills, which are valuable in any workplace. For example, mentoring a junior colleague can improve leadership and teaching skills, while volunteering for community service can enhance project management and teamwork abilities.

5. Increased Job Satisfaction

A workplace culture that promotes helping and cooperation can lead to higher job satisfaction. Professionals who engage in helping behaviours often feel more connected to their workplace and more valued by their peers. This sense of community can make their work feel more meaningful and enjoyable, reducing burnout and increasing overall job satisfaction.

6. Personal Growth and Self-Esteem

Helping others can contribute to personal growth by providing new perspectives and experiences. It can challenge professionals to step out of their comfort zones and develop new skills. Additionally, the act of helping can boost self-esteem and confidence. Knowing that they have made a difference can empower professionals and enhance their sense of self-worth.

7. Enhanced Problem-Solving and Innovation

Working with others to solve problems can stimulate creativity and innovation. When professionals collaborate and help each other, they can pool their knowledge and skills to develop more effective solutions. This collaborative approach can lead to new ideas and improvements that might not have been possible individually.

Practical Ways to Help Others

1. **Mentorship Programs**: Engage in formal or informal mentorship within the organization. Offer guidance, support, and advice to less experienced colleagues.

2. **Volunteering**: Participate in or organize volunteer activities. Many companies support corporate social responsibility initiatives that professionals can join.

3. **Peer Support Groups**: Create or join peer support groups where colleagues can share challenges and solutions, offering emotional and professional support.

4. **Knowledge Sharing**: Lead training sessions, workshops, or webinars to share expertise with colleagues. This not only helps others but also reinforces your own knowledge.

5. **Active Listening**: Simply being available to listen to colleagues' concerns can be immensely helpful. Offer a supportive ear and constructive feedback.

6. **Random Acts of Kindness**: Small acts, such as helping a colleague with a heavy workload, offering praise, or providing constructive feedback, can create a positive work environment.

As I complete writing my book, I want you to understand one universal law, that you are here to learn your lessons, the lessons could be hard for some, each one would have their own different lessons, each time you make your choice your life is going to transform in that manner, however if you tend to make repeated mistakes, you will always see a repeated patterns in your life.

It is important to own your responsibility towards your life instead of complaining, victimizing or seeking excuses.

Mindset, Skillset, Massive action will take you ahead in your life

Strong people Strive, Weak minded always loose

"If you can't fly then run, if you can't run then walk, if you can't walk then crawl, but whatever you do you have to keep moving forward." – Martin Luther King Jr.

"I wish you, the reader, excellent emotional, mental, and physical well-being. Keep striving for personal growth and self-improvement."

Connect With The Author

"I trust this book will serve as a valuable self-guide for you. If you're interested in continuing your learning journey with me and joining the Power of Emotional Healing program, please reach out using the link below. Share your details, and I will connect with you soon. Thank you!"

www.preetijoshi.com
www.listen2mee.com

Testimonies

"The voice of the customer is crucial for my personal growth and improvement. Here are a few pieces of feedback shared by my valued clients.

"Dr. Seema Girish, Asst. Vice president in Insurance organisation– Dubai

I understood more about Rebranding, the importance of communicating wisely, and how to help solve complex situations or projects using the DIPICTO principle. It's important to get the team to answer those and with brainstorming, we can find solutions to even toughest situations.

Coaching sessions with Preetiji is bringing big results in my daily life, both at home and work. I have become more positive and my communication has become less emotional which helps me to convey better & bring better results. Today I have learnt various ways by which I could generate opportunities for myself.

Dr Sejal Nikam, Dentist – Manchester UK

Coaching session with Preeti Mam have been very Useful. It opened my mind to the aspect and analysis of own self that I never would have thought on. The coaching sessions made me realize that I have manifested the current situation and that I can change it if I work on it. Preeti Mam has helped me to look at problems and career obstacles/patients in multiple perspectives i.e. Scientific as well as Metaphysical. I am seeing wonderful shifts in my reality and thank Preeti mam for all her help

Rajeev S Murthy, Regional Sales head, Bangalore - I have known Preeti Joshi for many years as motivator and a coach, Preeti is very empathetic and straight to the point during any crisis and a fallback guru, Preeti has guided me with utmost understanding and professionalism, I thank her for guiding me during my difficult times and help me overcome successfully.

Varsha, Boutique owner (Nagpur) - I where have has been misspelled taken healing sessions from Preeti mam since 2016, she has helped me heal from a changed illness and she has also has guided me and my family accurately, thank you for your timely guidance

Neeta singh Thakkur - I have enjoyed learning from Preetiji since 2022, she is knowledgeable in varied spectrum of subjects and she enthusiastically shares her knowledge, I have always looked forward for her coaching sessions and highly recommend to consult Preeti ji

Amita Joshi (Australia) - Discovering my patterns was interesting and inspiring, it was reassuring and it helped me find confidence to go through life chosen paths and finding purpose of my life, Preeti ji helped me navigate through matters of my health, career and family with more efficiency and grace, Preetiji is extremely gifted and talented individual, there was a very motherly nurturing and warm feel to the entire process. I highly recommend her for guidance, insights and healing. Thank you

Khushi Belani, Boutique owner (Goa) - Thank you Preetiji, you have been an incredible mentor and role model for me and I am also thankful for your guidance & coaching. I am very grateful for all the time and effort you put in to help us go through the right way, especially when my daughter Anusha started her new course in Mumbai, how well you guided all of us and now my daughter is doing well in her field, Thank you

- Journey Continues

www.ingramcontent.com/pod-product-compliance
Lightning Source LLC
LaVergne TN
LVHW061549070526
838199LV00077B/6968